T0318703

Cambridge Elements ≡

Elements in Political Economy
edited by
David Stasavage
New York University

LYNCHING AND LOCAL JUSTICE

Legitimacy and Accountability in Weak States

Danielle F. Jung

Emory University

Dara Kay Cohen

Harvard Kennedy School

CAMBRIDGE
UNIVERSITY PRESS

CAMBRIDGE
UNIVERSITY PRESS

University Printing House, Cambridge CB2 8BS, United Kingdom

One Liberty Plaza, 20th Floor, New York, NY 10006, USA

477 Williamstown Road, Port Melbourne, VIC 3207, Australia

314–321, 3rd Floor, Plot 3, Splendor Forum, Jasola District Centre,
New Delhi – 110025, India

79 Anson Road, #06–04/06, Singapore 079906

Cambridge University Press is part of the University of Cambridge.

It furthers the University's mission by disseminating knowledge in the pursuit of
education, learning, and research at the highest international levels of excellence.

www.cambridge.org
Information on this title: www.cambridge.org/9781108794473
DOI: 10.1017/9781108885591

First published 2020

A catalogue record for this publication is available from the British Library.

ISBN 978-1-108-79447-3 Paperback
ISSN 2398-4031 (online)
ISSN 2514-3816 (print)

Additional resources for this publication at www.cambridge.org/9781108794473

Lynching and Local Justice

Legitimacy and Accountability in Weak States

Elements in Political Economy

DOI: 10.1017/9781108885591
First published online: July 2020

Danielle F. Jung
Emory University

Dara Kay Cohen
Harvard Kennedy School

Correspondence for authors: danielle.jung@emory.edu and
dara_cohen@hks.harvard.edu

Abstract: What are the social and political consequences of poor state governance and low state legitimacy? Under what conditions does lynching – lethal, extralegal group violence to punish offenses to the community – become an acceptable practice? We argue lynching emerges when neither the state nor its challengers have a monopoly over legitimate authority. When authority is contested or ambiguous, mass punishment for transgressions can emerge that is public, brutal, and requires broad participation. Using new cross-national data, we demonstrate lynching is a persistent problem in dozens of countries over the last four decades. Drawing on original survey and interview data from Haiti and South Africa, we show that which actors provide governance is associated with perceptions of their legitimacy, and in turn how lynching emerges and becomes accepted. Specifically, support for lynching is most likely in one of three conditions: when states fail to provide governance, when nonstate actors provide social services, or when community members must rely on self-help.

Keywords: accountability, legitimacy, governance, community justice, lynching

ISBNs: 9781108794473 (PB), 9781108885591 (OC)
ISSNs: 2398-4031 (online), 2514-3816 (print)

Contents

1 Introduction: Local Justice, Legitimacy, and Accountability

It might not be the best justice, but this is justice.
— Focus group participant, Port-au-Prince, May 2017[1]

In many pockets of the world, justice is administered not in courtrooms by agents of the state, but rather by ad hoc groups of community members seeking to punish criminals and others who have offended local standards. Relatively minor crimes are brutally penalized by ordinary citizens, resulting in what amounts to capital punishment through astonishingly grisly means: beating, stoning, burning, and even decapitation are reported in some contexts.

Lynching – lethal, extralegal group violence, as defined in Section 1.1.2 – is a global political and social problem in the contemporary world. Several examples from recent years illustrate the widespread occurrence of lynching in countries and cultures around the globe, across the developed and developing worlds. In 2007, a suspected drug dealer was publicly tarred and feathered in broad daylight in Belfast, after local people became frustrated that police had failed to act on information about him selling illegal drugs.[2] In 2016, areas of Brazil were engulfed in a "lynching epidemic," mainly of perpetrators of petty theft, with an estimated average of one death by mob violence every two days.[3] In India, during the summer of 2018, the Supreme Court condemned a wave of lynchings, seemingly fueled by social media, in response to rumors of cow vigilantism, child abductions, and other crimes.[4] Finally, a focus group participant in Haiti relayed the following story to us:

> When I was young, someone stole a chicken. It was 10 o'clock in the morning on a Sunday. The people in the community grabbed the thief, put a tire on his head, and tied him up. I didn't stay to see what they did to him. They didn't know what he was going to do with the chicken – if he did it because he was hungry or was going to sell it. The thief was asking for forgiveness and understanding and said he was hungry, but the population was willing to kill him. But it was just a chicken![5]

The frequency and widespread acceptance of lynching in the modern world is both horrific and puzzling. In this Element, we examine the practice of lynching

---

[1] Focus Group 1, Port-au-Prince, May 15, 2017.

[2] "Tar and Feather Attack 'Barbaric,'" *BBC News*, 28 August 2007. http://news.bbc.co.uk/2/hi/uk_news/northern_ireland/6966493.stm.

[3] Cleuci de Oliveira in Fortaleza, "Brazil Grapples with Lynch Mob Epidemic: 'A Good Criminal is a Dead Criminal,'" *The Guardian*, December 6, 2016: www.theguardian.com/world/2016/dec/06/brazil-lynch-mobs-vigilante-justice-fortaleza.

[4] Dhananjay Mahapatra, "Mob Lynching: 'Draft New Legislation to Stop People Taking Law into Own Hands,'" *Times of India,* July 24, 2018: https://timesofindia.indiatimes.com/india/mob-lynching-draft-new-legislation-to-stop-people-taking-law-into-own-hands-says-sc-to-parliament/articleshow/65019261.cms.

[5] Focus Group 7, Port-au-Prince, September 23, 2019.

using multiple levels of analysis. At the cross-national level, we use an original dataset – the first of its kind – to document the global nature of the practice. As we describe in Section 3, we find high levels of lynching and related forms of mob violence in 46 countries between 1976–2013, as well as reports of lynching in more than 100 countries in the same period.[6] We show that some of the common explanations for lynching – such as lack of economic development and an absence of police presence – are not strongly associated with reports of lynching on the cross-national and local levels. The failure of these conventional wisdoms suggests there are important factors, other than poverty and the state's failure to provide policing, that drive the practice.

Tensions over perceptions of what constitutes appropriate punishments for crimes or social transgressions – and who should mete them out – are age-old problems.[7] Although some histories of lynching suggest the practice is unique to the American South in the nineteenth century, more recent studies have sought to place lynching in a global comparative and historical context, showing, for instance, that community killings and mob justice were not uncommon in both Czarist Russia and Imperial Germany (Berg and Wendt 2011: 2).[8]

We argue that a key feature of lynching centers on the politics of state and nonstate authority and legitimacy on the hyper-local level. As other scholars have maintained, lynching is not an isolated event but rather "predicated on localized notions of crime and punishment" (Berg and Wendt 2011: 13). The cross-national data presented in Section 3 serve to situate both Haiti and South Africa within broader global patterns. However, our goal in this Element is not to explore fully the roots of the cross-national variation; there are limits to what cross-national analysis can tell us about the emergence and persistence of lynching. Therefore, rather than asking why lynching is common in some countries and not in others, we instead turn to analyzing detailed data in one case where lynching is particularly widespread: Port-au-Prince, Haiti.

Haiti, where experts concur that lynching is one of the "central ... human rights concerns" (INURED 2017: 19), makes a good case for our analysis because it is a notoriously weak state with a number of competing actors.[9] We build on foundational work analyzing limited statehood and ungoverned spaces

---

[6] High levels of lynching are defined as a coding of 3 (massive) using our ordinal scale, as described in Section 3 and the Online Appendix.

[7] See Yates (2017) on lynching as part of the system of justice and as a tool of social control in pre-conquest Bolivia.

[8] For a global *historical* perspective on lynching, see Carrigen and Waldrep (2013) and Pfeifer (2017).

[9] While we argue that Haiti is critical and informative case, we cannot readily make relative comparisons with other cases (in terms of whether it is a hard or easy case for our theory) because similar data in other contexts have not yet been collected.

(e.g., Risse and Stollenwerk 2018a and 2018b) as well as research that takes nuanced views of sovereignty (e.g., Krasner 2004) to theorize how both state and nonstate governors interact with governance and accountability. This body of work is at the vanguard in theorizing how legitimacy might be generated by actors other than the sovereign territorial state – and how it may be accomplished short of conflict. In this Element, we explicitly examine conditions of limited statehood and de facto ungoverned territories within states – when the state and other nonstate actors fail to provide rules and order – to understand the conditions under which individuals take the mantle of justice and accountability into their own hands.[10]

In addition, existing data from Haiti (discussed in more detail later) clearly show that reported incidents of lynching are not correlated with state capacity on the local level (i.e., the presence of police). Although the presence of the UN stabilization mission in Haiti may arguably limit the generalizability of the case, our view is that it largely does not: first, because the UN is another governor that can, under some circumstances, exhibit state-like features, and second, because the UN is generally not widely trusted in the post–cholera epidemic era.[11] As a result, the UN is perhaps more similar to a nonstate armed group than it might be in another case. In any event, the UN peacekeeping mission ended in October 2019, and was replaced by a smaller political mission.[12]

Using micro-level data from Haiti, we explore the conditions that make the incidence of lynching *and* the broad acceptance of lynching more likely. We argue that which particular actors – in this case, the state, "gangs,"[13] or individuals – provide governance to the population predicts public perceptions of these actors' legitimacy, and can in turn explain when lynching is most likely to emerge. Specifically, we demonstrate that support for lynching is most likely under one of three conditions: when states fail to provide basic services; when gangs provide some services; or when no actor provides services and community members must rely on self-help. We also find that lynching is less likely to be supported when the state provides good governance, and thus enjoys strong public legitimacy. Lynching does not appear to be strictly tied to the presence of the state – that is,

---

[10] As we present in Section 2, we consider the full range of governance possibilities – from consolidated state, to nonstate (rebel or gang) order, to a total absence of either – in our theoretical account when we consider where local justice emerges and persists.

[11] In March 2017, there were large street protests demanding compensation for the victims of the cholera epidemic and that all UN forces leave Haiti, indicating a lack of confidence in the UN.

[12] Jacqueline Charles, "'A Historic Moment.' U.N. Establishes a Replacement for Departing Haiti Peacekeepers," *Miami Herald*, June 25, 2019: www.miamiherald.com/news/nation-world/world/americas/haiti/article231929473.html.

[13] As we discuss later, we use "gangs" in the Haitian context as an umbrella term for the several types of violent nonstate actors comprised of what are locally called *baz*, *bandi*, and *brigades*.

whether the police are patrolling – but rather to the quality of the basic public services that various actors provide and the legitimacy of these actors.

Overall, state legitimacy is most strongly affected by the state's own governance behavior. When states are repressive, abusive, corrupt, or ineffective, the public tends to view state institutions as illegitimate, and nonstate actors as more legitimate. When nonstate actors provide governance and social services, we find this increases perception of legitimacy *for those actors* – but has little or no effect on perceptions of state legitimacy. And when people receive services from no actor – neither the state nor gangs – the state's legitimacy generally remains stable while the legitimacy of gangs suffers.[14] Taken together, our results extend previous arguments about state legitimacy, and shed light on potential policy implications for states seeking to curb a rash of lynching: reducing citizen uncertainty about the sources of governance and providing reliable basic services may serve to mitigate or even halt support for and use of lynching.

1.1 Defining Terms and Concepts

Before proceeding further, it is useful to first define some of the terms and concepts we use in this analysis: vigilantism, lynching, legitimacy, and governance.

1.1.1 Vigilantism

The study of *vigilantism* is common in other disciplines, such as anthropology, history, and sociology, but far less frequent in political science, with some exceptions.[15] Unfortunately, across these diverse literatures, there is little consensus on how to define vigilantism. We follow Bateson (2019: 2) and define vigilantism as "the extralegal prevention, investigation, or punishment of offenses." Notably, Bateson's definition does not preclude state agents themselves from engaging in, tolerating, or condoning acts of vigilantism. In addition, her definition recognizes that "groups and individuals may engage in vigilantism habitually or sporadically" (Bateson 2019: 7). Like Bateson, we view lynching as a subcategory of vigilantism; albeit a less organized form, as we describe in Section 1.1.2. There are still many open questions about the conditions under which vigilantism is most likely to emerge. Some scholars

---

[14] In the Haitian context, we also examine the provision of services by a multitude of other actors, such as NGOs, the UN, and churches. As we show in Section 4, most respondents do not report receiving services from these groups, with the exception of water provided by NGOs. Of course, whether these groups are in fact providing services is distinct from whether respondents recognize the source of the services they receive. Our theory relies on respondents' *perceptions* of which actors provide governance outputs.

[15] See, for example, Goldstein (2003) in anthropology, Allen (2004) in history, and Godoy (2006) in sociology. Exceptions from political science include Reno (2011) and LeBas (2013).

argue that vigilantism typically emerges in environments characterized by insecurity, whether chronic instability due to war or periodic unrest caused by political change, disease epidemics, and natural disasters.[16] But these general hypotheses about predictors of vigilantism remain largely untested, mainly due to a lack of comparative data across cases.

1.1.2 Lynching

Our definition of *lynching* is lethal, extralegal group violence, perpetrated by ordinary people,[17] intended to punish offenses to the community; or, more succinctly, community-based capital punishment, sometimes called the "popular death penalty" (Jacobs and Schuetze 2011: 232). We base our definition on Berg and Wendt (2011: 5), who conceptualize lynching as "a form of extralegal punishment, usually entailing death or severe physical harm, perpetrated by groups claiming to represent the will of the large community." Building on this definition, we more specifically focus on *lethal* violence (or what can reasonably be expected to be lethal), and on the nonspecialist nature of the perpetrators. Lynching can be perpetrated using any type of method or weapon, including but not limited to beating, stoning, hanging, burning, or stabbing.

Lynching can be considered one type of "organized collective violence committed primarily by civilians" (Weintraub 2016: 5). Weintraub presents a useful typology that considers such violence along two dimensions: (1) the level of *organization* of civilian groups (which can either be informal groups that lack an official name and are mobilized on an ad hoc basis or formal groups with names, rules, and training provided to members) and (2) the *aim* (which can either be the control of the social order, such as policing homosexuality and dress, or the reduction of crime.) This ideal-type typology suggests a scope for the present analysis: we examine the emergence of informal, spontaneous, ad hoc groups of civilians seeking to reduce crime in their neighborhoods. We do not theorize or analyze the emergence of lynching by more formal vigilante groups, such as *brigades* in Haiti, which have a far higher degree of organization. For example, at times brigades notify city hall and police stations of their existence, issue identification cards and uniforms to members, and offer members training on policing practices. Unlike the ad hoc formation of lynching groups, some brigades use a form of conscription, in which each household must contribute a member.[18]

---

[16] For an example of this type of argument, see Édouard and Dandoy (2016: 2).

[17] By "violence by ordinary people," we mean violence not undertaken by the police or designated security forces but instead performed by mobs or vigilantes of ordinary citizens; incidents may be observed or tolerated by authorities but are not organized by them or with them (in contrast to civilian militias or formal vigilante groups, such as *brigades* in Haiti).

[18] See Édouard and Dandoy (2016) for a detailed analysis of *brigades* in Haiti.

We also distinguish lynching from other forms of public group violence that seek to control social order, such as antigay mobs and honor killings.[19] While these types of events can be observationally equivalent to lynching criminals, we do not focus on the punishment of "moral" offenses, but rather on interpersonal crime. Of course, these aims are difficult to separate in some cases. In our conception of lynching as a form of community justice, the purpose of the violence is to punish and deter perpetrators of *interpersonal community violence*, ranging from petty crime, such as property theft and pickpocketing, to more serious violent crimes such as rape and murder.[20] As we discuss in Section 3, in our cross-national data we find that the vast majority of reported lynching victims have been accused of a form of violence or crime against the community or one of its members, such as robbery or murder.

The emergence and persistence of this form of justice for quashing community violence is a clear indicator that the state is no longer the sole authority.[21] In previous scholarship on lynching, some observers understand lynching to be a form of "street justice" to fill in for state failure to properly police communities. In our research in Haiti, we find evidence that popular support for extreme violence as a punishment is largely because it may serve as a means to avoid reprisals, highlighting the lack of trust in state authority to curb crime. One scholar described this logic of deterrence to us: "The thing to do is to kill the thief before he comes back for you. If you don't kill them, you are putting yourself and your family in danger."[22] A focus group participant made a similar observation: "If you let the police come and arrest [a suspected murderer], he will go to jail probably. But as you know about our justice system, he will be free very soon. That is one of the reasons why this happens: the people kill the criminal so that they are sure he doesn't come back to get his revenge."[23] Édouard and Dandoy (2016: 20) echo this argument about lynching in Haiti, calling it "a permanent solution to the security threats and risks posed by bandits [because] it obliterates any hint or possibility of reprisals."

---

[19] While the research on these various forms of violence is too vast to cite here, see, for example, Franklin (2004) on antigay violence as a form of "participatory theater" and Chesler (2010) for an overview of trends in honor killing.

[20] The World Health Organization (WHO) distinguishes between *community* violence and *family* violence, the latter of which includes child abuse, intimate partner violence, and elder abuse. See "Definition and typology of violence": www.who.int/violenceprevention/approach/definition/en/

[21] Soifer (2012) also argues that lynching can serve as a proxy for low state capacity, and advocates measuring state capacity using a combination of the rates of lynching and violent crime, and private security per capita.

[22] Authors' interview with local scholar, August 7, 2018.

[23] Focus Group 8, Port-au-Prince, September 23, 2019.

Beyond the simple deterrence of future crime, other observers assign deeper political and symbolic meanings to lynching. Previous research on lynching in a historical, global context often understands it as a form of public protest in search of "certainty and security" (Jacobs and Schuetze 2011); individuals who are targeted may be scapegoats representing larger societal problems. For instance, Goldstein (2003: 23) analyzes a lynching in rural Bolivia and argues that the extreme mob violence in response to thieves is not an act of revenge by "enraged sociopaths" but rather "a form of political expression for people without access to formal legal venues [and] . . . a communication of grievances" about the failure of the state's legal order. From the more symbolic perspective, "[l]ynchings express people's desire to fill a gaping void of justice seeking" (Jacobs and Schuetze 2011: 231) left by absentee states.

Participants in lynching are not proto-rebels and, generally, have no underlying agenda to overthrow the state. Rather they are often seeking to improve their quality of life using a mode of self-governance. In the case of Bolivia, lynching comprised part of the "insistence on citizenship" by indigenous people, who had been long neglected by the state. While the salient cleavages in Haiti are more economic than racial (or religious), a similar argument can be made about why the prevalence of lynching seems highest in the poorest areas, and support for lynching is highest among those most ignored by the state in terms of governance provision.[24] As Berg and Wendt (2011: 14) argue, "Supporters of popular justice are not opposed to the state per se; rather they are critical of its actual performance."[25] Unlike rebel challengers, the purpose of lynching is not to overturn the state but rather to "compel the state to live up to its own claims of legitimacy" (Goldstein 2003: 24).

The mitigation of crime and deeper symbolic meanings are not necessarily mutually exclusive. As we also find in the case of Haiti (see Section 4), Goldstein argues the police in Bolivia are viewed as corrupt and the justice system is essentially unavailable to marginalized people. In this way, lynching is both a practical solution to the problem of crime *and* serves as an expressive form of political violence.

1.1.3 Lynching in the US Context

Lynching has a particular historical meaning in the United States, which we briefly acknowledge here, in part because the American experience is perhaps

---

[24] However, "governance provision" does not necessarily include police presence, a point we describe later; the presence of police is correlated with *increased* lynching in the Haitian context.

[25] We find evidence that the state is implicitly the preferred provider in Haiti, using a survey experiment presented in Section 4.

the most familiar case.[26] Scholars estimate that thousands of people were lynched in the United States in the nineteenth century, peaking between the 1880s and 1930s. The majority of lynching victims were African-American men in the US South. However, blacks were not the sole victims of lynching; other victims included whites, Native Americans, Mexicans, Chinese, and Sicilians (Pfeifer 2017). A 1905 sociological study of US lynching, one of the earliest scholarly treatments, understood lynching to be particular to the United States, calling it America's "national crime" and claiming that such violence is "found in no other country of a high degree of civilization" (quoted in Berg and Wendt 2011: 1). Indeed, the very term "lynch" is thought to have its origins in the extralegal courts of the era of the American Revolution, which were presided over by Colonel Charles Lynch of Virginia, who organized unauthorized punishments of criminals in violation of "Lynch's Law."

Much of the social science literature on lynching in the United States has debated its root causes, with a particular focus on whether poverty was a central driver. The "frustration-aggression" hypothesis posited that the frustration of whites during economic downturns lead to aggressive targeting of minority groups. In an early test of this hypothesis, Hovland and Sears (1940) found suggestive supportive evidence and argued that there were fewer lynchings during periods with better economic conditions. Decades later, Green et al. (1998) overturned these results, finding they did not replicate when using more sophisticated statistical techniques. Further, once the data were extended, there was no increase in lynching during the Great Depression, the greatest macroeconomic downturn in US history. As a result of this work, economic drivers have been largely dismissed as a cause of lynching in the United States.

More recent literature has also diverged from the earlier studies arguing American exceptionalism. Contemporary scholars increasingly recognize that lynching and related practices have occurred in many countries, and throughout history (e.g., Berg and Wendt 2011; Pfeifer 2017). Scholars acknowledge that lynching in the US South meets standard definitions of lynching – including our own – as it was undoubtedly "lethal, extralegal group violence, perpetrated by ordinary people."

However, the US case also has some unique properties; for example, its focus on *racist* social control (not social control in general, which, as previously argued, is a common aim of collective violence committed by ordinary people). Also unusual about the US case is the fact that accusations of the rape of white women by black men was a frequent precipitating crime. But scholars argue that

---

[26] The literature on this topic is vast; one of the most widely cited is Tolnay and Beck (1995).

these motivations of racism and rape are not universal reasons for lynching. Racist hatred of blacks cannot explain all of the lynching incidents in the United States; for example, whites and non-black minorities were lynched as part of the system of "frontier justice," in areas lacking a formal justice process during roughly the same time period. Further, racial terror explanations fail to account for lynching in other countries and in other time periods where lynching is more commonly employed as a tool of the weak and powerless. As Berg and Wendt (2011: 13) argue, "In other parts of the world, poor people's struggle against perceived injustices and self-defense against rampant crime seem to have been much more important than racial solidarity."

1.1.4 Legitimacy and Governance

There are many definitions of *legitimacy* and legitimate rule. We define legitimacy as "rightful rule,"[27] following Lake, who conceives of political authority as resting "on the collective acceptance ... of the governor's right to rule." Central to the concept is that authority, and the "rightfulness" of a ruler, rests on some broad, local, "collective acceptance" of the leader or on a set of potentially informal rules. These ideas can be traced back to Hobbes, who acknowledged that the Leviathan's power comes from "the opinion and belief of the people."[28] Because our theory embraces the potential for authority in situations where the state has little, uneven, or even no authority at all over the people and where other nonstates actors – such as gangs – may have significant authority, we rest our argument on these more popular notions of authority, rather than legally or institutionally derived authority.[29]

This informal rightful rule can help to explain the emergence and persistence of the practice of lynching. The sense of broad, highly localized support for, and participation in, acts of popular justice is a way of both legitimizing and entrenching the practice. The accountability that emerges from a local population in the case of lynching is to that local population, rather than only to a feudal, state, or religious process of authority and accountability.

Finally, legitimacy is closely linked to governance. *Governance* is a very broad term; it can mean, for example, "the sum of the many ways individuals and

---

[27] Lake (2010: 592) relaxes authority for the purposes of thinking about moving from state-based definitions of legitimacy to conceptualizing global governance, at a level above states. We adopt a similar shift, albeit downward, and use theories initially designed to explain international relations between states to analyze microdynamics at the subnational level. For a discussion of multilevel legitimacy, see Scharpf (2007).

[28] Hobbes, quoted in Williams (2006: 265) as quoted in Lake (2010: 592).

[29] In Section 4, we employ multiple measures of state legitimacy, including ones that measure respondents' senses that the state's power to enforce contracts should be supported and/or expanded (including willingness to be taxed, support for expanding the armed forces, and willingness to go to state authorities to adjudicate disputes).

institutions, public and private, manage their common affairs" (Commission on Global Governance 1995: 2).[30] We define governance as authority in a social relationship in which one actor will voluntarily comply with decisions issued by another.[31] We explore governance via the provision of a variety of services at the micro level, from security – the service most commonly associated with the state – to basic social services including water, trash collection, and road maintenance. In our central theory (Section 2), we argue that the provision of governance can determine whether the provider is viewed as legitimate, and show evidence of this link using our survey data from Haiti (Section 4).

1.2 Consequences of Lynching

Having clarified some of the core terms and concepts, we now turn to examining some of the effects of extrajudicial justice. While lynching can have the benefit of curbing or deterring crime and of expressing political grievances, there are several aspects of lynching that make its emergence and persistence particularly costly for the communities that engage in it. These costs include the rapid speed at which incidents of lynching take place, leaving communities without the ability to investigate prior to punishment; the possibility that lynching is plausibly linked to other negative social outcomes; and the disproportionality of the punishment relative to the crime. Each of these represent significant costs that communities face when lynching becomes common, and can serve as a partial explanation for why lynching might not become even more widespread. When lynching becomes accepted, this can be a sign that the community has determined the benefits of lynching outweigh the costs, entrenching a system of justice that is outside the scope of the law and the state.

First, episodes of lynching often happen quickly, with swift, even spontaneous, movement from accusation to "conviction" to punishment, leaving little time for the investigatory stage between.[32] The speed and informality of the process can lead to false "convictions" and unwarranted punishments. For example, in a case of mistaken identity in Bolivia, a group of children were targeted. As summarized in the US State Department reports: "On April 7, police in Cochabamba broke up three separate lynching attempts to kill up to ten

---

[30] This report is quoted in Kahler and Lake (2003: 7).

[31] This conception follows Kahler and Lake (2003: 7–8), on whose work on global governance we build by turning a similar lens *down* rather than *up*.

[32] A focus group participant in Port-au-Prince, Haiti, acknowledged how sensitive the practice is to emotion, and that use of this form of justice makes one vulnerable to these swings: "The population will get angry, when you give yourself justice you might get punished in the future" (Focus Group 1, Port-au-Prince, May 15, 2017).

persons for robberies. In one incident a crowd beat a group of six children ranging in age from fourteen to seventeen, only to find hours later the children were not the thieves" (US State Department Human Rights Report, Bolivia 2009). Beyond potentially punishing the wrong person, the rapidity of lynching exacts societal-level costs of inconsistent and unpredictable justice, which in turn contribute to perceptions of insecurity and uncertainty, both important factors in explaining the persistence of lynching. Such uncertainty may create further difficulties in establishing and enforcing reliable expectations, which are at the heart of the rule of law.

A second cost related to lynching is that the existence and acceptance of the practice can cascade to other negative social outcomes. Lynching can be manipulated by savvy entrepreneurs and exploited to target vulnerable, politically unpopular, or ostracized groups or individuals. In our cross-national data collection, we find the great majority of reported victims of lynching and related practices were persons suspected of criminal activities, including robbery, sexual assault, and cattle rustling. However, lynching can sometimes provide cover for personal revenge under the guise of "mob justice."

In our data, there are some reports of social misfits and strangers unknown to the community who were the targets of mob violence. For example, there were at least sixteen women killed on suspicion of practicing witchcraft in Kenya in 1998,[33] and there have been periodic episodes of lynching in response to rumors of vampires in Malawi.[34] In Mozambique, elderly women, who by virtue of surviving younger family members and avoiding the HIV epidemic, have been accused of witchcraft and lynched (Jacobs and Schuetze 2011). Recently in India, there have also been examples of pernicious rumors about cow theft, kidnapping, or other crimes perpetuated through social media, leading to a spate of lynching deaths.[35] Beyond the immediate social consequences, there is evidence that lynching can have negative long-term social and political consequences for a community, a theme to which we return in the Conclusion (Section 5).

---

[33] State Department Human Rights Report, Kenya 1998.

[34] "Vampire Scare Triggers Mob Violence, Prompts U.N. to Pull Staff," *NBC News*, October 10, 2017, www.nbcnews.com/news/world/vampire-scare-triggers-mob-violence-prompts-u-n-pull-staff-n809386.

[35] Geeta Anand and Suhasini Raj, "Rumors on WhatsApp Ignite 2 Mob Attacks in India, Killing 7," *New York Times*, May 25, 2017: www.nytimes.com/2017/05/25/world/asia/india-vigilante-mob-violence.html. While some blame social media itself for these lynchings, others point to deep-seated social cleavages and the fact that the rates of social media penetration are not closely correlated with spikes in lynching violence (e.g., Alexis C. Madrigal, "India's Lynching Epidemic and the Problem with Blaming Tech," *The Atlantic*, September 25, 2018: www .theatlantic.com/technology/archive/2018/09/whatsapp/571276/.)

A third cost of lynching is its inefficiency: relatively minor crimes such as theft are often punished severely and disproportionately, frequently with capital punishment. One reason for such brutality is deterrence. As one focus group participant put it, "If we see someone steal something small, we know that he might steal something bigger than that in the future. There is a Haitian expression: if you steal an egg, you could steal a cow." A second participant responded, "I would 100 percent support a decision to kill someone who came into my community to commit a crime. He can be an example that it should never happen again in the community."[36]

Community members recognize the absence of appropriately functioning state mechanisms that should hold perpetrators of crime accountable, or should punish them in ways that are deemed acceptable. The selection of an extremely brutal form of violence may result from a hope that the community develops a reputation for having a zero-tolerance attitude toward crime. It also can serve as an ominous warning to those considering committing crimes about how the neighborhood treats those who injure its members or violate community norms. Under conditions of extreme poverty, the simple act of petty theft may be viewed as deeply destabilizing to its victims. Therefore, the deterrence of thieves through lynching is one way to relieve the crippling anxiety of vulnerable populations about economic insecurity.

There are numerous other plausible reasons for the brutality of lynching, although an analysis of individual participants' motivations is beyond the scope of this Element. Lynching can involve "overkill" or "violent display" (Fujii 2017): bodies are sometimes burned or otherwise violated after the fact. One reason may be "appetitive aggression," or positive feelings associated with perpetrating violence that can provide individuals with resilience in the face of adversity (Weierstall and Elbert 2011). Another related possibility is that lynching provides an opportunity for a small number of violence-seeking types to participate in a "dark carnival" of violence that would otherwise be socially unacceptable (Mueller 2000: 60). As one anthropologist of Haiti told us, lynching sometimes happens because "[The perpetrators] want to beat the hell out of someone and this is an opportunity to do it without repercussions." A focus group participant described that when people in his community participate in lynching a criminal, "they are usually very happy, joyful, gleeful."[37] These descriptions echo one of the most well-cited books about lynching in the US South, *A Festival of Violence* (Tolnay and Beck 1995), which raises the possibility that lynchings were

---

[36] Focus Group 8, Port-au-Prince, Haiti, September 23, 2019.
[37] Focus Group 8, Port-au-Prince, Haiti, September 23, 2019.

concentrated in the summer months because they served as a form of recreation, as daring and entertaining as the circus.

The potential for a mismatch between the punishment that the state provides and that which the community prefers has persisted for centuries.[38] For instance, in *Utopia*, More (1845: 24–25) notes the practice of capital punishment for thieves. While More writes about the state meting out extreme punishment rather than citizens as we do in this Element, he notes the perverse incentives that may result:

> *[I]t is plain and obvious that it is absurd, and of ill consequence to the commonwealth, that a thief and a murderer should be equally punished: for if a robber sees that his danger is the same – if he is convicted of theft, as if he were guilty of murder – this will naturally set him on to kill the person whom otherwise he would only have robbed, since, if the punishment is the same there is more security, and less danger of discovery … ; so that terrifying thieves too much provokes them to cruelty.*

In the sections that follow, we analyze situations in which there is popular agreement that an incident of community violence – be it petty theft or a violent crime such as rape or murder – must be punished, and an attendant belief that the state is not willing or able to perform its role in holding the perpetrator of the offense accountable in ways that community deems appropriate.

We argue that any ambiguity about the ultimate political authority in a territory can create significant uncertainty in the populace, and lead to the endogenous emergence of local solutions to impose order. The legitimacy of state justice and accountability mechanisms can erode at a number of junctures, all resulting in the potential for lynching. For instance, citizens may trust local police and believe the police are not supported by the broader justice system (i.e., police co-perpetrate or are present at lynchings); police may be seen as barely competent, and citizens do not trust the greater justice system (i.e., citizens kidnap and lynch individuals who are already in police custody); police may be entirely uninvolved, and citizens do not trust the greater justice system (i.e., citizens lynching in the absence of police). Lynching is often broadly accepted – but is also a suboptimal, inefficient, parallel practice to the state's justice system. In other words, lynching can emerge when the state is not necessarily completely absent, but rather, is deeply mistrusted or seen as ineffective on the local or state level.

---

[38] However, this mismatch can work in reverse as well: deleterious practices can also emerge when states are perceived as too *lenient* on perceived criminals and the community prefers a far harsher punishment than the one the state is likely to provide. The estimated 4,743 lynchings of African-Americans in the US South fall into this category. See, for example, Jamiles Lartey and Sam Morris, "How White Americans Used Lynchings to Terrorize and Control Black People," *The Guardian*, April 28, 2018: www.theguardian.com/us-news/2018/apr/26/lynchings-memorial-us -south-montgomery-alabama.

Our theory can help to resolve the puzzle of why lynching is observed in areas *with* a heavy police presence as well as in remote, rural areas. A United Nations study found that rates of reported lynching in Haiti are highest in areas with the greatest police presence (MINUSTAH 2017). As we observed in our fieldwork in Haiti, despite their proximity to agents of the state or the UN security forces, residents of slum areas have no expectation that the state or the UN will respond to calls for assistance. And when the state does respond, the people have little faith that the perpetrator will face appropriate sanctions – largely due to agents and institutions within the justice system being vulnerable to bribery and corruption. This same logic is at work when citizens break into police stations to punish accused criminals who are already in custody. Thus, a hypothesis (that we do not fully explore here, due to data limitations) is that lynching emerges where state *legitimacy* is lacking, not necessarily where state *presence* is lacking.[39]

1.2.1 Lynching as a Form of Brutal, Public, Collective Violence

Lynching is a form of group violence, in which ordinary people – who would otherwise not be violent or enjoy watching violence – may spontaneously participate in or witness extraordinary brutality. Here, we briefly highlight several aspects of lynching that pertain to the group public nature of the violence.

First, on the individual level, collective participation in killing protects participants from a sense of direct personal responsibility, easing the potential emotional trauma of such intimate violence. A similar logic underpins firing squad executions in which multiple shooters are used so that the "true" executioner is never known.[40] Participants can be known to have done their gruesome social duty, but not have to shoulder alone the psychological weight of having been the killer.[41] The group nature of the violence also helps to overcome (or at least to lower) an individual's personal reluctance to participate, in essence solving a collective action problem.

---

[39] While state capacity may be correlated in some contexts with state legitimacy, in other contexts, such as Haiti, it is not.

[40] "Utah Brings Back Firing Squad Executions; Witnesses Recall the Last One," *NPR*, All Things Considered, April 5, 2014. www.npr.org/2015/04/05/397672199/utah-brings-back-firing-squad-executions-witnesses-recall-the-last-one. Additionally, see an extensive literature on the "Firing Squad Synchronization Problem," following Myhill (1957) (Moore 1964).

[41] A similar logic can explain perpetrators' perceptions of participation in gang rape; see Cohen (2016).

Second, from a legal perspective, large groups of participants make it difficult for the state to prosecute any individual perpetrators. For instance, in the case of Haiti, perpetrators of lynching experience near-total impunity, due to the difficulty of identifying individuals who participated, challenges in gathering evidence of the crime, and even the refusal of police to execute warrants (MINUSTAH 2017: 21). Only one lynching case in Haiti has *ever* resulted in a conviction; the sentence in that case was a single year in prison (MINUSTAH 2017: 24).

Further, the method of killing (for example, stabbing, stoning, setting on fire, or beating while restraining the victim) typically means there is no single identifiable executioner who can be held legally accountable. Beyond the perpetrators, there are typically many witnesses to lynching; an estimated 1.5 million people in Brazil have personally witnessed episodes of lynching.[42] Under some legal codes, including Haiti's, witnessing a killing, without intervening on behalf of the victim or failing to report the crime to police, is considered a crime. As is evident in anecdotes from Haiti and from patterns apparent in our cross-national data, identifying, arresting, and trying participants in lynching are extraordinarily difficult tasks for state justice systems, particularly where these systems are weak. As mentioned previously, India is currently debating whether to impose harsher laws for participating in lynching, but strict laws – even when they exist – are difficult to enforce in practice. As Édouard and Dandoy (2016: 20) write, lynching involves the tacit agreement and approval of entire communities. They call the lynching process a "secret pact and code of silence."

Finally, in the absence of a single governing authority – the conditions under which lynching is most likely to emerge – methods that require group participation may increase the perception of mass support (or rightful rule, as we defined earlier) for the judgement of the guilt of the victim and the justness of the punishment. The widespread use of modes of execution that require many participants is likely a critical factor in establishing broad community support for the practice. When many individuals are required to perform the act of lynching, this imbues the practice with a particularly local form of legitimacy, creating a fertile setting for its repeated use.[43] Broad participation signals the punishment has social legitimacy (or at the very least, some direct support and broad acquiescence), similar to the way low turnout rates may signal a lack of a democratic or popular mandate in an election. As one anthropologist of Haiti told us, "During a lynching, there is broad public support for what they are

---

[42] Samantha Pearson and Luciana Magalhaes, "In Latin America, Awash in Crime, Citizens Impose Their Own Brutal Justice," *Wall Street Journal*, December 6, 2018: www.wsj.com/articles/in-a-continent-awash-in-crime-citizens-impose-their-own-brutal-justice-1544110959.

[43] As we explore in Section 3, we see evidence of lynching being a *persistent* (rather than episodic) phenomenon in many regions of the world.

doing . . . [with] broad support for egregious violent acts, it becomes legitimate. People of all ages, both sexes."[44]

As we discuss in Section 4, we find that nearly half of our respondents in Haiti support lynching: 49 percent of respondents in Port-au-Prince find lynching a thief to be an appropriate punishment and 43 percent find it to be an appropriate response to murder. In Section 3, we report similar, although more extreme, results from a study of Khayelitsha township outside of Cape Town, South Africa; we find 64 percent of respondents report lynching a thief to be an appropriate punishment and 75 percent found it to be an appropriate response to murder. In both cases, while there is some variation in degree, there is clear public support for a community response to community crimes.

1.3 Outline for the Element

In this Element, we explore two broad questions: (1) *What are the social and political consequences of poor state governance and low state legitimacy?* (2) *Under what conditions does lynching – lethal, extralegal group violence to punish offenses to the community – become an acceptable practice?*

In Section 2, we present our central theory. We link governance output to its consequences on perceptions of actors' legitimacy, and finally link perceptions of legitimacy to support for lynching. We discuss the very important role of nonstate actors as possible governance providers. While we focus particularly on gangs as the main nonstate competitors to the state, our theory may be generalized to include insurgent groups, rebels and other types of political challengers, as well as to areas of state retrenchment in difficult-to-govern regions. Finally, we offer hypotheses and observable implications for the dependent variables of legitimacy and support for lynching to be explored in later sections.

In Section 3, we use original cross-national data to demonstrate the reporting and persistence of lynching and related practices during the past four decades. These data show that lynching is not merely a problem of weak states, and that it is not closely associated with poverty or lack of development, both common arguments. We also show patterns in the practice of lynching that help illuminate the practice: relative prevalence across space and time, the reported method of execution, and the precipitating crime. However, because lynching is the result of variation in micro-level political contestation, there are limits to what cross-national analysis can offer. We offer a brief examination of original survey data on the approval of lynching from Khayelitsha township in South Africa, highlighting the value in exploring subnational variation.

---

[44] Authors' interview with local scholar, August 7, 2018.

In Section 4, we turn to the micro level and leverage original survey and focus group data collected during fieldwork in Port-au-Prince, Haiti, in 2017 and 2019. Using these data, we study the linkages between governance output, perceptions of legitimacy, and support for lynching. In line with our theory, we find that both the providers and quality of governance predict perceptions of the providers' legitimacy, and can in turn explain when lynching is viewed as acceptable. Specifically, we demonstrate that support for lynching is most likely in one of three conditions: when the states fails to provide services, when gangs provide some (but not all) services, or when no actor provides services and neighbors must rely on each other in a self-help system.

Throughout our surveys in South Africa and Haiti, we ask about *support* for – rather than participation in – lynching due to concerns about reporting biases. Survey respondents are unlikely to admit to participating in lynching. Even the term "participation" is ambiguous and can suggest a wide range of activities, from actively killing to restraining a victim to watching without interfering. Because community involvement is so central to the success of lynching, we argue that a measure of approval for lynching is the best method for assessing support for lynching.[45]

In Section 5, we explore some of the implications for our analysis for policy and theory. We conclude by considering how the practice of lynching might be curbed, and which policies are most likely to be successful. We also discuss how our findings speak to broad questions in political economy about state formation and decay, as well as the sources of accountability and justice, and suggest a number of promising future paths for research.

Taken together, the global data and the detailed case study evidence show that lynching is a serious problem in many parts of the contemporary world. Our goal with this Element is to propose a theory of why lynching emerges, how lynching interacts with governance, and some of the consequences of lynching for state legitimacy.

2 Toward a Theory of Local Governance, Legitimacy, and Lynching

> *"The word justice should be removed from the Haitian dictionary; whether political, social, or economic, there is no justice."*
>
> *–Focus group participant, Port-au-Prince, Haiti[46]*

---

[45] The question of the extent of direct participation in lynching is certainly of great interest and has not yet been studied (to our knowledge). However, for the present analysis, we are interested in how perceptions of the practice of lynching take hold more broadly in society. Given budgetary constraints restricted us to a relatively small sample size, we felt it was more important to address the latter issue, rather than estimate the extent of direct participation.

[46] Focus Group 8, September 23, 2019.

We turn now to our central theory on the emergence and persistence of lynching. We begin by considering the theoretical foundations of the state, governance, and authority. We then turn to the core argument: we link governance output to its consequences on perceptions of actors' legitimacy, and finally tie perceptions of legitimacy to support for lynching. We discuss the role of nonstate actors as possible governance providers. Finally, we develop hypotheses for the dependent variables of legitimacy and support for lynching, and consider their observable implications, to be explored in later sections.

2.1 Foundational Notions of State Accountability

One of the most essential functions of the sovereign territorial state is ensuring accountability for violations of norms and laws. But what happens to dispute resolution, justice, and accountability when the formal state is illegitimate, weak, or completely absent? The sovereign territorial state is widely assumed to have a monopoly on both the use of violence and legitimacy within its borders (Weber 1918).[47] The notion that this authority cannot be split among actors stems from Grotius, who noted "sovereignty is a unity, in itself indivisible" (quoted in Keene 2002: 43–44).

Since Westphalia, scholars of political authority and international relations have tended to treat sovereignty and legitimacy as analytically uniform, and constant within a given territory.[48] However, this consolidation is far from universal in practice (e.g., Krasner 1993). While a wealth of scholarship has tracked the process of state formation within this model, recent research has sought to understand the voluntary and involuntary cedes of state functions and authorities to other entities (e.g., Keohane 2002; Krasner 1999; Lake 2009). Much of this literature is focused on transfers from states to other states in more and less hierarchical arrangements between similar entities, such as informal empires or protectorates (Lake 1999).

Current literature analyzes transfers to dissimilar, nonstate actor types, in which some functions of the state are shifted to an international entity or organization, such as in peacekeeping missions (e.g., Krasner and Risse 2014). Research over the past two decades demonstrates that there are many instances in which challenges to state legitimacy and sovereignty come from a substate actor seeking to revise the current boundaries of state control (i.e., a violent challenge to the integrity of the state, as in a civil war). As Osorio et al. (2019: 5) write, "In weak states, state presence is unevenly distributed

---

[47] See also Spruyt (1994) for a nuanced treatment of the emergence of the sovereign territorial state.

[48] The most extreme characterization of this approach is neorealism, but most theories and paradigms in international relations start (and often end) with the state as the central actor in whom authority resides.

geographically and, in many cases, state institutions are subject to capture by well-organized non-state actors with access to the tools of violence."

Legitimacy and even the identity of the "rightful ruler," may vary significantly within the boundaries of the state. Most commonly, direct challenges come in the form of insurgent or rebel organizations, which seek to replace the state as the legitimate political authority within a territory. These rebel governors establish elaborate institutions to facilitate governance and to establish legitimacy (e.g., Arjona 2015; Jo 2018; Mampilly 2011). With challenges of this type, wholesale shifts in the identity of the rightful ruler may emerge, in which a nonstate monopoly is consolidated. For example, a network of local courts enforcing Sharia law called the Islamic Courts Union brutally governed large parts of Somalia for several years.[49] ISIS is also reported to have effectively governed Mosul, with residents acknowledging the establishment of services and a monopoly over law and order as an improvement over the uncertainty of a weak Iraqi state.[50]

2.2 Nonstate actors providing governance

Our argument combines work on legitimacy, in which international relations scholars have focused primarily on the state, with a growing literature on nonstate governance in civil wars. Illicit organizations such as rebel groups often set up local institutions. Groups undertake the costly process of institution building to enable them to direct their members more effectively to achieve their goals (Berman 2011; Bahney et al. 2013; Shapiro 2013; Shapiro and Jung 2014; Johnston et al. 2016). However, these groups also serve as competitors with the state in governance, by creating an alternate law and order (Loyle and Binningsbø 2018), organizing elections (Cunningham et al. 2018), and offering basic services such as trash collection, education, and medical services (Cammett 2014; Heger and Jung 2017; Wagstaff and Jung 2018).

Rebels, terrorists, and insurgents are inherently political organizations; however, these are not the only illicit groups that govern. Many scholars have drawn analogies between rebel and terrorist organizations and other types of criminal groups such as drug trafficking organizations and gangs (see Kenney 2007; Lessing 2015, 2017; Phillips 2015; Levitt and Venkatesh 2000; Cammett and MacLean 2014). We depart slightly from those studying rebel governance and other violent *political* actors, in that the primary focus

---

[49] Edmund Sanders, "Islamists Bring Order to Somalia but Justice is Far from Uniform," *Seattle Times*, October 15, 2006: www.seattletimes.com/nation-world/islamists-bring-order-to-somalia -but-justice-is-far-from-uniform/.

[50] Rukmini Callimachi, "The Caliphate," *New York Times*, 2018. "www.nytimes.com/interactive/ 2018/podcasts/caliphate-isis-rukmini-callimachi.html.

of our analysis is *criminal* actors who have taken on significant governance activities to facilitate their goals. We join other scholars who have called for a recognition that non-state armed groups can "originate and thrive in non-war situations" (Rodgers and Muggah 2009: 301). In recent years, political scientists have taken this call seriously by making moves to expand and redefine the boundaries between political and criminal actors, and to advocate for the inclusion of criminal violence in studies of political violence (e.g., Arias 2017; Barnes 2017; Lessing 2015; Moncada 2019).

A result of studying criminal actors is that we can focus exclusively on popular legitimacy, rather than potentially conflating it with a population's support to replace or establish a new state by political actors. In Section 4, we study criminal gangs in Port-au-Prince, Haiti, which provide services and govern many micro-areas in the capital city. This type of organization is analytically useful because, while they undeniably have political *effects* on the Haitian state, gangs are not primarily political organizations in the conventional sense.

Exploring the dynamics of criminal actors' governance can inform and complement the literature on rebel governance and institutions. Because the scope of our study is ad hoc anti-crime lynching, our argument differs from a small emerging consensus on the growth of formal vigilante groups and militias. Vigilantism is predicted by prior experiences during periods of civil war, during which civilians are socialized into a system of militarized control over each other (e.g., Bateson 2017; Osorio 2019). In the Haitian case, we explore similar civilian mobilization – albeit less formalized – in the *absence* of a recent history of full-scale civil war.

2.3 Core Argument

We argue that monopoly over the ultimate political authority and legitimate governance is, inherently, indivisible. While states often delegate provision of services to other entities – such as religious institutions, NGOs, IGOs, and INGOs – what distinguishes these situations from those in which the state's legitimacy is waning is that the state is perceived as retaining a monopoly on the de facto rights of control.[51] In short, the state can *rightfully* revoke this delegation. For instance, private prisons in the United States are the agents of the state entity that delegates and can remove authority, but the state government remains ultimately, legally responsible (Gunderson 2018).

What emerges in such situations are pernicious practices to fill the gap in perceived public order neglected by the state. When there is ambiguity over the

---

[51] Lake (1999: 26) describes these as the "residual" rights of control: the party with the ability to make decisions when contracts or agreements are imperfectly specified or incomplete.

rightful ruler, or a lack of state monopoly on rightful rule, the practice of extrajudicial community justice and accountability is most likely to emerge.[52] We contend that mass participation marks this practice with a stamp of grassroots legitimacy. In principle, elements of the state may be delegated either upward (i.e., to an international organization) or downward (i.e., to a subnational organization, such as a local NGO or religious organization). However, in states where the hold on legitimacy is tenuous but the state is nonetheless still seen as the primary locus of such delegation, authority is neither certain nor universally accepted. Such settings are where lynching is likely to emerge and to persist.

Our argument proceeds in two steps, as is displayed in Figure 2.1 below. In the first step, we link the quality and availability of governance output by the state, nonstate actors, and community members to perceptions of legitimacy of state and nonstate actors. In the second step, we link perceptions of legitimacy to the likelihood that community members will express support for lynching. Below, and in our empirical tests of the theory in Section 4, we follow the links across each type of

	Quality of Governance		Perceptions of Legitimacy		Expected Change in Lynching Support
State governance	**Good state governance** (security and all basic service provision; always a monopoly)	→	State: high Non-state: low	→	Decreased
	Poor state governance (due to repression/abuse or inefficiency/corruption; uncertainty; no monopoly)	→	State: low Non-state: low	→	Increased
Non-state governance	*Good political non-state governance* Rebel governance *(security and some basic service provision; possibly short of a monopoly; less uncertainty in controlled areas)*	→	*State: low Non-state: high*	→	*Decreased*
	Good criminal governance Gang governance (security and some basic service provision; always short of a monopoly; uncertainty)	→	State: no effect Non-state: high	→	Increased
Self-help	**Poor state and non-state governance** Neighborhood self-help (total self-help system; no monopoly; uncertainty)	→	State: low (or no effect) Non-state: low	→	Increased

Figure 2.1 Summary of Central Argument and Predictions: Governance, Legitimacy and Lynching

Note: We focus on the Gang governance row in this Element; we do not test the Rebel governance row.

---

[52] Other practices consistent with ambiguity might include favoring rotating credit associations over banks, water associations, or heavy reliance on community norms over laws.

governance output through legitimacy to understand the conditions under which lynching receives more or less public support.

2.3.1 Linking Governance Outputs to Perceptions of Legitimacy

We analyze shifts from state control to other actors by examining violent nonstate actors – in our case, criminal gangs – who do not necessarily seek a revision of formal central control of the state, but who nonetheless can and do locally govern. We argue these governance activities, which include the provision of basic goods and services, have substantial consequences for understanding the micro-foundations of legitimacy and sovereignty. The literature has focused almost exclusively on substate challenges to state legitimacy through violent conflict. Risse and Stollenwerk (2018b) are among the few to argue these revisions can happen *outside* the context of war, and beyond the goal of the nonstate actor seizing central control of the state.

A lack of state legitimacy is a very general context; it is one that has long existed in stateless societies and continues to exist today in cases where the formal state lacks control over some parts of its territory. As we show, the legitimacy of states *within* their borders is not uniform; this variation can be marked by nonstate challenges to rule in the form of civil war, insurgency or terrorism, or can be the result of more mundane seizures of the state's responsibilities, as in the case of gangs.

When states are inadequate, or corrupt, citizens lose trust in many aspects of the state. As state governance output erodes, so too does the core authority of the state, resulting in the lack of a state monopoly on the residual rights of governance. When this happens, citizens turn to local and even hyper-local (neighborhood-level) actors, social organizations, and practices to manage their daily challenges. The endogenous emergence of institutions and dispute resolution in settings where the state is absent is well studied (Anderson and Hill 2004; Ellickson 1994; Lansing 2006; Leeson 2007). But we show that these institutions can also emerge in settings where the state, or other actors such as gangs or rebels, may be actively trying to consolidate control.

As is displayed in Figure 2.1, we outline five potential states of the world in terms of governance output.

1. Good state governance: Good state governance leads to a monopoly on authority by the state and strong state legitimacy. In this case, the state provides satisfactory governance, and we predict that the state will enjoy a high degree of public legitimacy. Nonstate actors, such as gangs or rebels, will not be viewed as legitimate authorities.

The lack of a state monopoly on authority can result from three situations: (1) the state fails in some critical duty in the eyes of the governed (what we might think of as "poor behavior" by the state); (2) some other actor works to challenge or supplant the state's monopoly on governance, but does so incompletely (what we might think of as "good behavior" by a nonstate actor); or (3) both state and nonstate governance are weak, and citizens are forced to rely on self-help governance by neighbors. These scenarios are not necessarily mutually exclusive, but they show an ideal-type pathway for how these steps connect.

2. <u>Poor state governance</u>: When the state provides poor governance output, its monopoly on legitimacy is undermined. This poor performance may be due to repression by the state, or the state may be corrupt or simply inefficient. In any case, the state's legitimacy suffers, and nonstate actors' legitimacy is expected to increase. (Nonstate legitimacy may be expected to increase even more if the nonstate actor is also providing some governance.) We theorize that the public's preference for the state to have a monopoly is so strong that state legitimacy is difficult to degrade unless the state itself performs poorly. Poor state governance is the *only* condition in which state legitimacy suffers. In these circumstances, support for and trust in those actors to whom a legitimate governor would delegate authority, such as the police or a national army, are likely to be seen as ineffective.

   Additionally, the mechanisms in place to enforce property rights and adjudicate interpersonal disputes are no longer trusted, and therefore less likely to be used. We find support for this hypothesis; as we show in Haiti with a short priming experiment and focus groups interviews in Section 4, there is a clear underlying preference among the public that the state *should* have a monopoly.

3 and 4. <u>Good political and non-political nonstate governance</u>: It is well established that nonstate actors provide some governance outputs in the form of basic service provision. But there are two types of nonstate actors: (1) politically motivated, nonstate actors who seek central control of the state, such as rebel groups, and (2) non-political, nonstate actors, such as criminals or gangs, who may control local areas but do not have designs on state control. Politically motivated nonstate actors, such as rebels, who provide competing governance in the form of basic services may gain legitimacy at the expense of the state (e.g., Arjona 2015; Stewart 2018). However, nonpolitical, nonstate actors, such as gangs, are likely to have a less pronounced effect on state legitimacy through service provision and governance activities.

While nonpolitical, nonstate actors can successfully offer some forms of governance, this provision is always short of a monopoly; there is only so much that a nonstate actor can reasonably accomplish. As Lessing and Willis (2019: 8–9) argue, "criminal governance is often narrow . . . when it extends over civilian life, it does so unevenly. A gang might monopolize drug sales, prohibit property crime, and punish civilian contact with police, but leave realms like informal transport, disputes, and electoral politics unregulated." Thus, it is unlikely a nonpolitical, nonstate actor governs robustly in the absence of a state that has withdrawn, or a state that never fully consolidated control.

Further, while nonstate actors can (and do) step into the void, the quality and quantity of justice and accountability services provided may not be equivalent to what a state could provide or may have provided in the past. Nonstate services may be fewer, of a lower quality, or less consistently available than services provided by a functioning state. While this may be preferable to a lack of services, it creates inefficient provision, and significant uncertainty for the populace. For instance, there are increased search costs – effort spent on seeking alternatives – for individuals who must seek services (sometimes even the same services) from multiple actors.

Of course, any competition over which institutions rightfully rule means the state has lost its monopoly on ultimate legitimacy. But it is likely that gangs have a less corrosive effect on state legitimacy than would a rebel group. (We do not test this proposition in the current analysis.) Because the scope of the Element focuses on nonpolitical nonstate actors, we argue that when a nonpolitical nonstate actor provides some governance, its authority and thus its legitimacy increases. Meanwhile, the state's legitimacy remains unchanged (or is only weakly diminished) because of its privileged position as the implicit rightful ruler.

5. <u>Self-help governance</u>: When neither the state nor nonstate actors are providing services, citizens are completely neglected. Both entities are weak and practical authority comes from neighborhood collective action. In this most extreme case, we again predict that the legitimacy of these neglectful actors will suffer. In such cases, citizens do not have faith in any political authority to hold perpetrators accountable.

We next detail three situations that can give rise to the emergence of lynching in the interstitial spaces where legitimacy is imperfectly consolidated, either by the state or a nonstate entity; see final column of Figure 2.1. Whether due to state corruption, a nonstate actor providing services, or a total absence of governance that gives rise to self-help local governance by neighbors, the state's ultimate authority is fundamentally challenged. When citizens lack a single actor who has a monopoly on authority, they feel anxiety and uncertainty. Multiple providers of governance can create ambiguity about who is best to serve in this role.

In other words, cobbled-together, ad hoc governance may be negative for social welfare. Beside lynching, other outcomes of ad hoc governance can include forestalling of the establishment of trade, inconsistent enforcement of property rights, exploitation, human rights abuses and general instability, including abuses within the home. The emergence of these practices highlight the decay of the rule of law and also make the reestablishment of rule of law all the more difficult.

Lynching gains popular legitimacy because it requires the participation of (and is often witnessed by) many community members. For example, Schwartz (2008: 38–42) describes an incident in a Haitian village in which hundreds of villagers – "500 men, dozens of boys and several women" – hunted down and eventually stoned a young man to death after he accidentally shot an older man in a scuffle. Any measures to curb violence like this would need to supplant and replace popular, communal, and local consent, so efforts to mitigate the practice face many obstacles. In Section 5, we return to the issue of curbing lynching.

2.3.2 Linking Perceptions of Legitimacy to Support for Lynching

Perceptions of legitimacy are associated with support for lynching. Uncertainty over the lack of a monopoly can cause people to turn to self-organized dispute adjudication in the form of lynching, in which ordinary people – often spontaneously – mete out lethal punishment for interpersonal crimes. In brief, the formation and decay of legitimacy may affect or inhibit popular support of lynching. As we lay out in Figure 2.1, we predict that attitudes toward legitimacy will be associated with support (or lack of support) for lynching.

2.4 Testable Implications

Our argument leads to a series of testable hypotheses, described here in stages and then explored in subsequent sections. Table 2.1 summarizes the hypotheses as well as observable implications.

Table 2.1 Summary of Hypotheses and Observable Implications: Governance, Legitimacy, and Support for Lynching

Dependent Variable	Relevant Actor(s)	Hypothesis	Observable implications (Tested in Section 4)
Legitimacy	*State and nonstate actors*	H1. Perceptions of an actor's governance output are associated with perceptions of their legitimacy.	*State actors:* • Respondents who report the state is effective are more likely to report positive indicators of state legitimacy. • Respondents who report the state is ineffective are more likely to report negative indicators of state legitimacy. *Nonstate actors:* • Respondents who report the nonstate actor is effective are more likely to report positive indicators of nonstate legitimacy. • Respondents who report the nonstate actor is ineffective are more likely to report negative indicators of nonstate legitimacy.
	State actors	H2. Perceptions of good governance by state actors are associated with decreased nonstate legitimacy.	Respondents who report the state provides good governance will be more likely to report negative indicators of nonstate legitimacy.
		H3. Perceptions of poor governance by state actors are associated with increased nonstate actor legitimacy.	Respondents who report the state provides poor governance will be more likely to report positive indicators of nonstate legitimacy.

Nonstate actors	H4. Perceptions of good governance by nonstate actors are *not* associated with indicators of state legitimacy.	Respondents who report the state provides good governance will be no less likely to likely to positive indicators of nonstate legitimacy.
Neighbors	H5. Reliance on neighbors for governance (in the absence of either state or nonstate actors) are associated with decreased nonstate legitimacy and are not associated with indicators of state legitimacy.	Respondents who report relying on neighbors for good governance will be more likely to report negative indicators of nonstate legitimacy and will be no less likely to report positive indicators of state legitimacy.
Support for Lynching — *State actors*	H6. Perceptions of the legitimacy of the state are inversely associated with approval of lynching.	Respondents who report *negative* assessments of state legitimacy will be *more likely* to report approval of lynching. Respondents who report *positive* assessments of state legitimacy will be *less* likely to report approval of lynching.
Nonstate actors	H7. Individuals who view nonstate actors as legitimate are more likely to approve of lynching.	Respondents who report positive assessments of nonstate actor legitimacy will be more likely to report approving of lynching.
Neighbors	H8. Individuals who rely on neighbors for governance are more likely to approve of lynching.	Respondents who report greater reliance on self-help governance by neighbors are more likely to report approving of lynching.

2.4.1 Hypotheses on the Link between Quality of Governance and Attitudes toward Legitimacy

We first hypothesize that perceptions of an actor's effectiveness in governance – whether a state or a nonstate actor – is directly related to that actor's legitimacy. These perceptions are likely to vary by individual: in many settings, particularly in the developing world and in countries that are challenging to govern, governance is not uniform within the territory.[53] Some aspects of the state may work well for some, while others feel neglected or ignored. If our central argument is correct, we should expect to see a direct relationship between individual-level perceptions of the quality of governance and attitudes about the legitimacy of the actor providing the governance.[54] In short, reporting that an actor is generally effective at governance will be associated with reporting of positive indicators of that actor's legitimacy; conversely, reporting an actor is ineffective is likely to be associated with decreased legitimacy.

- H1. Perceptions of an actor's governance output are associated with perceptions of their legitimacy.[55]

We expect the benefits of good state governance to extend beyond assessments of the state itself. Specifically, in contexts where the state is seen to be a good governor, the legitimacy of nonstate actors decreases.

- H2. Perceptions of good governance by state actors are associated with decreased nonstate legitimacy.

Next, we hypothesize that poor or ineffective state governance create an opportunity for nonstate governance, leading to greater legitimacy for nonstate actors.

- H3. Perceptions of poor governance by state actors are associated with increased nonstate actor legitimacy.

---

[53] These perceptions also likely vary by the distance to the capital or seat of power, and the nature of the terrain; however, we are unable to test these geographic predictions using the survey data we collected in Haiti because all respondents are essentially equidistant from the capital.

[54] In our Haiti survey, we operationalize perceptions of government effectiveness through a variety of proxy measures, such as respondents' expressed trust in the police. We operationalize indicators of state legitimacy as respondents' support for paying taxes to the state, preference to use state mechanisms (rather than gangs or neighbors) to resolve disputes, and support for the reinstatement of the Haitian National Army; see Section 4.

[55] Additionally, we expect, as a validity check, to see attitudes about violent actors who provide services to increase positively as they provide more services.

As we argued earlier in the section, a state's monopoly on legitimacy can be eroded by another *political* actor offering itself up as the rightful ruler, outside the bounds of regular political competition. In the case of rebel groups, secessionist or irredentist movements, this can happen wholesale, in a zero-sum manner, eroding the state's legitimacy. In instances of criminal or other illicit groups such as gangs, however, the state's primacy may remain largely unscathed. We hypothesize that *nonpolitical,* nonstate actors offering governance in the form of goods and services should result in positive indicators of that actor's legitimacy, but not necessarily decreased perceptions of state legitimacy; the state is still seen as the actor who ought to be doing governance activities.

- H4. Perceptions of good governance by nonstate actors are not associated with indicators of state legitimacy.

Finally, when neither state nor nonstate actors provide good governance, neighbors must turn to each other for self-help. Under these conditions, we theorize that neighborhood governance implies a decrease in nonstate legitimacy and, as above, has little effect on state legitimacy, though it is likely quite low in such circumstances. While it may still be the case that public perception is that the state ought to be the governance provider, it is also likely that the state is largely irrelevant to those who have been abandoned by all actors. While we do not predict a sizable influence of self-help governance on perceptions of state legitimacy, this does not imply state legitimacy is high; rather, we do not expect a significant additional decrease.

- H5. Reliance on neighbors for governance (in the absence of either state or nonstate actors) is associated with decreased nonstate legitimacy and is not be associated with indicators of state legitimacy.

2.4.2 Hypotheses Linking Perceptions of Legitimacy to the Approval of Lynching

State malfeasance, neglect, illicit governance, or neighborhood self-help governance may erode the legitimacy of the state on the individual level. The emergence of lynching represents a second stage of the erosion of legitimacy: it is a mechanism outside state institutions and authority. As a result, we hypothesize that lynching should meet with higher rates of public approval in places where legitimacy has eroded from an actor's monopoly (either state or a nonstate actor).

First, with respect to state legitimacy, we expect approval of lynching and perceptions of state legitimacy to be inversely related.

• H6. Perceptions of the legitimacy of the state are inversely associated with approval of lynching.

We expect that respondents who report negative assessments of state legitimacy will be more likely to report approval of lynching. Conversely, we expect that respondents who report *positive* assessments of state legitimacy will be *less* likely to report approval of lynching.

Turning to the condition when nonstate actors enjoy high legitimacy, what emerges is a complicated governance environment. In this context, the state is likely failing to provide robust services and governance; as a result, we expect individuals who report high nonstate actor legitimacy are also more likely to approve of lynching.

• H7. Individuals who view nonstate actors as legitimate are more likely to approve of lynching.

Our final prediction focuses on the link between neighborhood governance and lynching. In these pockets, many citizens turn to hyper-local self-help, and increased reliance on their neighbors for nearly all their needs. As this reliance deepens, the legitimacy of neighborhood governance should increase,[56] and we predict that approval for lynching, a community-level solution to violence, will increase.

• H8. Individuals who rely on neighbors for governance are more likely to approve of lynching.

We summarize these core hypotheses below in Table 2.1. We test these hypotheses and explore their observable implications we examine using subnational data from Haiti in Section 4. We first turn to examining patterns of lynching on the cross-national level.

3 Lynching Around the World: Cross-National Evidence

Lynching and related practices are common in many parts of the contemporary world. In this section, we use an original, cross-national dataset to describe the global prevalence during a nearly forty-year period. We then turn to describing a series of distinct patterns of lynching, including the identities of the

---

[56] Because this type of governance is so decentralized, we measure only whether respondents receive services from neighbors rather than directly measuring the legitimacy of neighborhood self-help.

victims and perpetrators, the reported precipitating cause of the violence, and the method of execution. While developing a full explanation for the cross-national variation in use of lynching is beyond the scope of this Element, we conduct an initial analysis of the cross-national correlates of lynching, shedding light on the external validity of some of the factors on the subnational level later in the Element.[57] We also briefly consider two common alternative explanations for lynching and show that they fail to explain the locations where lynching is most frequent. Finally, we leverage original subnational evidence from South Africa to highlight an environment with high rates of local support for lynching. The correlates of lynching approval in South Africa emphasize the importance of subnational data collection and serve as a prelude to our more detailed analysis of Haiti in Section 4.

3.1 A Note on the Data Source

To underscore the scope and scale of the practice, and to show its use in contexts where legitimacy and accountability are relatively weak, we created an original cross-national measure of lynching and related practices using the US State Department Human Rights Country Reports (hereafter, State Department reports).[58] Each report details physical integrity rights violations, such as torture, disappearances, and abuses by state forces and in conflict zones, as well as violations of other rights (e.g., labor, civil, political, women's, sexual and religious minorities, and children's rights). The State Department reports are widely seen as one of the most comprehensive and thorough reflection on the status of rights and liberties detailed in the Universal Declaration of Human Rights (UDHR) and other integral human rights documents, and have been used by many scholars of human rights to code different categories of violations across time and space (e.g., the Political Terror Scale (PTS) (Gibney et al. 2018) and the Sexual Violence in Armed Conflict (SVAC) dataset (Cohen and Nordås 2014)).[59] Presently, the reports cover 196 countries, more than similar yearly

---

[57] For an analysis of cross-national survey data on support for mob violence, see Cooper and Wilke (2018) which compares Uganda, Tanzania, South Africa, Papua New Guinea, and the United States.

[58] The State Department reports are congressionally mandated, begin coverage in 1976, and are issued annually to cover human rights practices in every country in the world (except the USA itself). These reports are a standard annual source in quantitative analyses of human rights, and have been converted into searchable text files by Fariss et al. (2015), which we use in the proceeding analysis.

[59] For sexual violence in particular, scholars have found that the State Department reports cover more violations than do the other two reports (Cohen 2016) and, as Cohen et al. (2012) argue, is the "most comprehensive currently available single source for cross-national comparisons ... " ("Is Wartime Rape Declining on a Global Scale? We Don't Know – And It Doesn't Matter," November 1, 2012, Dara Kay Cohen, Amelia Hoover Green, and Elisabeth Wood. *Political*

reports by Human Rights Watch or Amnesty International. Given the scope of the coverage and its widely recognized utility, we rely on the State Department reports as the main source for the analysis in this section.

Collecting systematic cross-national measures of lynching is challenging for several reasons, primarily because of reporting biases. First, because these acts can take place where democratic institutions, such as a free press, may be the least robust, they are unlikely to be covered by local newspapers. When lynchings are reported in local media, there may be strong incentives to misrepresent the facts surrounding the case, either to protect the perpetrators or to excuse the police who failed to act. As with civil war violence, the incidents of lynching most likely to be included in news reports are those that occur in urban areas. And the most extreme attacks – the most violent or the largest crowds of perpetrators and witnesses – are the ones most likely to be covered by newspapers or NGOs concerned about the practice (e.g., Davenport and Ball 2002).

For these reasons, it is most accurate to consider these cross-national data a measure of the *reporting* of lynching and related practices rather than a direct measure of the underlying incidence of lynching. However, we checked our data against existing anthologies of cases of contemporary lynching and generally found close agreement.[60] In sum, although the data we use in this section are likely incomplete, they are the first of their kind, and enable an initial analysis of where and when lynching was reported around the world.

3.2 Variables Coded

Because there are a number of common terms used to describe the phenomenon of lynching as we have defined it in Section 1, we coded mentions of the following terms, what we refer to collectively as "lynching and related practices": *lynch, community justice, mob justice, vigilante,* and *vigilantism.*[61] In addition to coding whether lynching and related practices were reported, we also coded information about the method of killing or attempted killing, the identity of the victim, the motives for the lynching, and other salient details. We code only actual physical violence, not threats. Finally, we created a measure of

---

Violence @ a Glance: http://politicalviolenceataglance.org/2012/11/01/is-wartime-rape-declining-on-a-global-scale-we-dont-know-and-it-doesnt-matter/.)

[60] For example, South Africa, Benin, Mozambique, Brazil, Indonesia, Guatemala, Angola, and Kenya are all mentioned in Berg and Wendt (2011) and Indonesia, India, South Africa, and Israel/Palestine (lynchings in the occupied territories from the 1980s onward) are included as cases in Pfeifer (2017) as countries with episodes of lynching in the modern era.

[61] Our research assistants extracted from the Farris et al. data the country-years that featured the search terms, and then hand-coded the relevant text from each report. We next created qualitative summaries of the reports of lynching and related practices for each country in which at least one search term was mentioned at least once.

prevalence, coding reports of lynching and related practices on an ordinal scale from 1 to 3: from isolated reports to reports of widespread or massive events.[62] In this section, we review these patterns, providing insight into how lynching has taken shape around the world.[63]

3.3 Global Prevalence of Lynching and Related Practices

Using the annual State Department reports, we searched the reports from 1976–2018 for mentions of lynching and related practices. Figure 3.1 displays all countries where lynching or a related practice were ever mentioned. It is notable that these practices were reported in almost every region in the world. During the study period, 102 countries had at least one mention.

Because the United States is not included in the State Department's reporting on human rights practices, we are unable to include the United States in this analysis; however, there are several well-known incidents that would be included if we were to code the United States, such as the 1981 lynching of Michael Donald in Mobile, Alabama (often called "the last lynching" because Donald's was one of the final deaths to occur by hanging), and the 1998 dragging death of James Byrd, Jr. by white supremacists in Jasper, Texas.

Lynching and Related Practices
■ Present

Figure 3.1 Presence of Lynching and Related Practices Worldwide, 1976–2013

Source: US State Department Human Rights Country Reports.
Note: The USA is not coded; it is not included in the US State Department reports.

---

[62] Our scale was adapted from a similar process of coding of wartime rape, using the same source (Cohen 2013; 2016). For a detailed description of the coding methodology, please see the Online Appendix.
[63] Summary statistics are reported in Table A.3 in the Online Appendix.

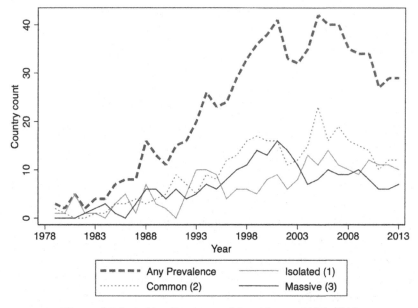

Figure 3.2 Lynching Reports and Prevalence, 1976–2013

3.3.1 Variation in Time and Severity

Having established that lynching is common in many regions of the world, we turn to examine variation over time. The thick dashed line in Figure 3.2 shows the frequency of country-years in which lynching and related practices, at any prevalence level, was reported. In total, we find 789 country-years in which lynching and related practices were reported. Reports of lynching and related practices generally increases significantly from the late 1970s through the end of the study period (2013). However, this may not indicate that the practice of lynching became more common. This upward trend may be due to better documentation of the practice, rather than an increase in the practice on the ground. Kathryn Sikkink (2017) calls this the "information paradox," which suggests that the process of exposing harms makes them appear to be getting more severe.

We next turn to analysis of prevalence over time, using the ordinal coding of prevalence. Lynching and associated practices are common and are consistently reported at all levels of prevalence (the three thin lines in Figure 3.2). In particular, forty-six countries experienced "massive" (level 3) lynching (the dark, solid line in the figure) in at least one year. Among these cases, at the highest level of prevalence are South Africa and Haiti, our two case studies in this Element. Approximately one-third (n=231) of the country-year observations with any reported lynching activity experienced it at this highest level. Although there are some notable dips in prevalence, all three levels generally increase over time.

In Figure 3.3, we examine the data by country, highlighting cases where lynching has been particularly prevalent.[64] The figure shows the top ten countries in terms of reports containing the most mentions of keywords over the period of study, tracking our measure of prevalence of lynching over time. We observe a number of patterns of temporal variation. Some country reports consistently mention lynching throughout much of the study period (e.g., Jamaica and Guatemala), while others had no mentions at all until the mid-1990s (e.g., Ecuador). Among these countries, only Guatemala and Brazil had reports before 1983, while every country had at least some reports in the final five years of the study period. Most countries experienced variation in the prevalence of lynching over the period of study: all countries except Jamaica record each of the three levels of prevalence, including the highest. Some countries, such as the Philippines, experience consistent, high-intensity reports (level 3) for over a decade of the period of study.

3.3.2 Victims

Available evidence suggests that the vast majority of both victims and perpetrators of lynching are men. We coded any reports that explicitly mentioned a female victim of lynching. A total of 22 percent (191/869) of country-years with reports of lynching mentioned female victims (note that we code the country-year as the unit of analysis, not the number of victims; one report in a particular country-year might mention numerous victims or incidents).[65]

Examples of female victims of lynching include the Benin (2013) report, which notes the following incident involving a female thief: "On April 30, local residents of Doko-Agbongnizounhoue, in the commune of Toviklin, intercepted a man and a woman who were suspected of stealing a motorbike. The crowd beat and burned the two suspects to death." Another example from Vietnam (2001) reports the severe beating of two

---

[64] This figure displays the ten countries with the most frequent keyword mentions. For a description of the top twenty countries – as defined by number of mentions of keywords – see Table A.1 in the Online Appendix.

[65] Figure A.1 in the Online Appendix displays the frequency of female victims of lynching and related practices.

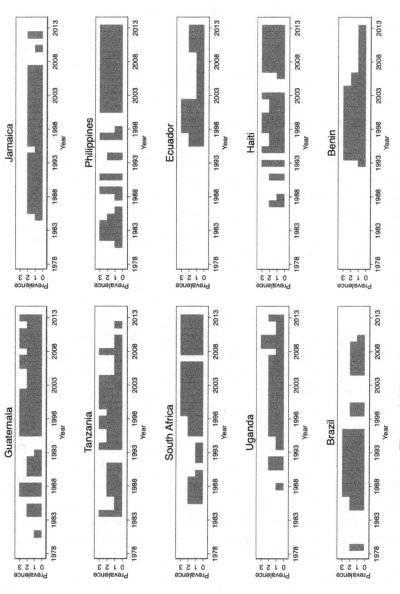

Figure 3.3 Prevalence of Lynching in Selected Countries

women who had attended Protestant religious services. Finally, in Papua New Guinea (2013), a woman was "beheaded in front of her community after being accused of sorcery."

Some of the incidents involving female victims involve gender-specific community violations, such as being a victim of rape or incest, or being accused of adultery.[66] These cases punish the *victim* of a crime and are more in the realm of social control than crime mitigation, placing them outside the scope of our theory. The 2011 report for Bangladesh notes a case of a fifteen-year-old girl who died after being whipped "at least 50 times" because she was "found guilty of adultery after she was raped by a relative" following a "village-based arbitration." By our definition, this incident describes social policing rather than control of community crime, the focus of our main theory. Below, we separately coded mentions of rape as a precipitating incident to the lynching, but do not disaggregate instances of punishing the victim from those that punish the perpetrator.

3.3.3 Precipitating Causes

We coded mentions of any proximate causes of the reported lynching episodes; common crimes included murder, kidnapping, theft, and rape. Of country-years that report episodes of lynching and related practices, about 13 percent mention murder as a precipitating cause, 7.5 percent mention property crime, 9 percent mention theft, and 5.5 percent mention kidnapping. While only four country-years contain clear evidence of honor killing, 6.5 percent of country-years that report episodes of lynching mention rape in the descriptions.

In the Figure 3.4, we present four common categories of crime that reportedly precipitated the lynching violence, over time.

3.3.4 Method of Execution

We now turn to analyzing the method of execution, if mentioned, in the State Department reports. While many reports of lynching have only brief descriptions, some methods are common within and across cases. As we show in

---

[66] While rare, there are some reports in the news of the opposite: men accused of rape being lynched by women. In one such incident in India, 200 women stabbed a local gang leader to death; he had terrorized their community by raping local women. Raekha Prasad, "'Arrest Us All': the 200 Women Who Killed a Rapist," *The Guardian*, September 16, 2005: www.theguardian.com /world/2005/sep/16/india.gender.

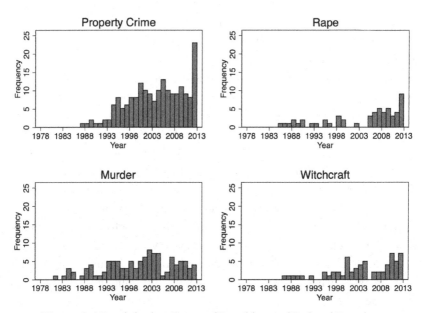

Figure 3.4 Precipitating Cause of Lynching and Related Practices

Figure 3.5 (in which the unit of analysis is the keyword mentioned), by far the most frequently mentioned method of execution is beating (far left bar), followed by burning (second bar from left, with dashed outline).[67] Shootings are far less common, with fewer than 100 mentions in our data, followed closely by stoning. Hanging and hacking/knife-related execution are the least common forms. As we noted in Sections 1 and 2, many of these modes of execution involve a large number of participants, and are intensely violent. It is consistent with our theory that these executions gain popular legitimacy as a form of accountability based on being public acts of violence with many witnesses, and use methods that enables many within the local neighborhood to take part in meting out justice.

3.4 Explanations for Cross-National Variation

While we do not explore these explanations at length, we briefly consider two conventional wisdoms for why lynching is common in some countries but not in others: poverty and weak rule of law. While the top quartile of high-income

---

[67] In the data from Haiti, there are many reports where execution is by one of these common methods, and the body is later burned; see Section 4.

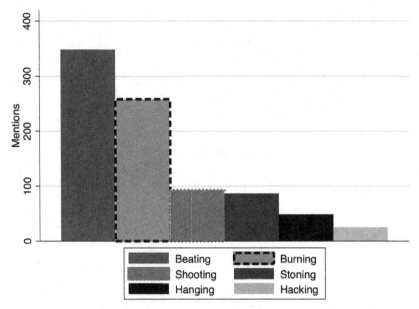

Figure 3.5 Reported Methods of Execution by Lynching

countries were least likely to feature reports of lynching (with only about 5 percent of all reports), there is little difference between the bottom three quartiles, each of which comprised roughly 30 percent of the reported lynchings by country-years.[68] Even this simple breakdown provides initial suggestive evidence that a state's level of poverty is not closely associated with reports of lynching, casting doubt on a powerful conventional wisdom that dictates that lynching is the exclusive purview of poor countries.

Weak rule of law is another factor thought to be associated with reports of lynching. Figure 3.6 shows the linear conditional correlations between various measure of rights, civil liberties, and the rule of law and our coding of prevalence of lynching and related practices, all drawn from the Varieties of Democracy (V-Dem) data project (Coppedge et al. 2018). We find that equality before the law and individual liberties,[69] the strength of local government,[70]

---

[68] Figure A.2 in the Online Appendix displays the breakdown of lynching years by WDI development indicators.

[69] The equality before the law and individual liberties index is a measure of, "To what extent are laws transparent and rigorously enforced and public administration impartial, and to what extent do citizens enjoy access to justice, secure property rights, freedom from forced labor, freedom of movement, physical integrity rights, and freedom of religion?" (Coppedge et al. 2018).

[70] The local government index is a measure of, "Are there elected local governments, and – if so – to what extent can they operate without interference from unelected bodies at the local level?" (Coppedge et al. 2018).

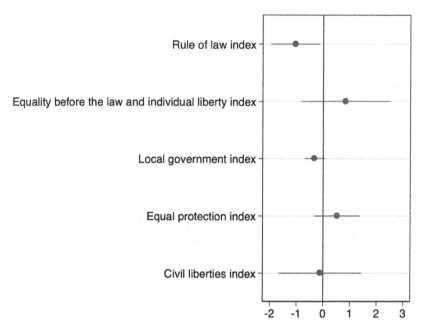

Figure 3.6 Rights, Liberties, Rule of Law and Lynching

Sources: US State Department Human Rights reports and Varieties of Democracy (V-Dem) variables

equal protections,[71] and the extent to which civil liberties are respected[72] are not associated with reports of lynching. However, we find that the rule of law[73] is negatively associated with lynching. In other words, having a weak rule of law is positively correlated with increased reports of lynching. This result is generally supportive of our central argument, highlighting that lynching can emerge in a variety of governance settings, not merely in low-capacity and poorly governed states.

Taken together, these correlations show that there are limits to what state-level analysis can offer. What is necessary is detailed subnational data, a task we turn to more completely in Section 4. But first, here, we use original survey data from South Africa to provide an initial exploration of the correlates of support for lynching.

---

[71] The equal protection index is a measure of, "How equal is the protection of rights and freedoms across social groups by the state?" (Coppedge et al. 2018).

[72] The civil liberties index is a measure of "To what extent is civil liberty respected?" (Coppedge et al. 2018).

[73] The rule of law index is a measure of, "To what extent are laws transparently, independently, predictably, impartially, and equally enforced, and to what extent do the actions of government officials comply with the law?" (Coppedge et al. 2018).

3.5 Evidence of Support for Lynching from South Africa

South Africa is a case in which lynching is reported to be common and persistent; it is one of the cases with the most consistent reports of lynching and related practices over the study period (see Figure 3.3). It is also a case, similar to Haiti, where lynchings are often spontaneous, rather than organized by a vigilante group.

To understand the degree of popular approval of lynching, we conducted a small survey of 516 adult residents of Khayelitsha township in Western Cape, between August 9 and October 4, 2017, using similar indicators to our Haiti study (discussed in Section 4).[74] Khayelitsha is among the most violent areas in the country; it ranked sixth in the country in terms of reports of murder to police.[75] It is also an area marked by numerous reported cases of lynching in recent years, including dozens that took place in a designated area called the "field of death," an abandoned soccer field.[76]

To gauge public support, we asked two separate questions regarding lynching, with response options in brackets:

- **Approval of Lynching for Property Crimes:** "What would you think if your neighbors killed a thief as punishment?" [*This is definitely an appropriate punishment; This might be an appropriate punishment; This is never an appropriate punishment.*]
- **Approval of Lynching for Murder:** "What would you think if your neighbors killed a killer as punishment?" [*This is definitely an appropriate punishment; This might be an appropriate punishment; This is never an appropriate punishment.*]

We find approval of lynching is widespread among respondents in Khayelitsha. In our sample, 63 percent of respondents thought it might be or definitely is appropriate to punish a thief in this manner, while 75 percent of respondents thought it might be or definitely is appropriate to punish a killer in this manner. That the vast majority of our respondents in

---

[74] Respondents were sampled at transit and commerce points. Our sample consisted of 516 adults (257 women and 259 men), all surveyed by an interviewer of the same gender. The survey was administered by and in collaboration with Ikapadata and Ikamva Youth.

[75] Jenna Etheridge, "Top 10 Areas You Are Most Likely to Be a Target of Violent Srime in SA," New24, September 11, 2018: www.news24.com/SouthAfrica/News/top-10-areas-you-are-most-likely-to-be-a-target-of-violent-crime-in-sa-20180911.

[76] Geoffrey York, "Vigilante Killings on the 'Field of Death' in South African Township," *Globe and Mail*, February 22, 2014: www.theglobeandmail.com/news/world/vigilante-killings-on-the-field-of-death-in-south-african-township/article17052460/.

Table 3.1 Support for Lynching in Khayelitsha Township, South Africa

		Definitely or might be appropriate to lynch killer		Definitely or might be appropriate to lynch thief
No	25%	(65% female/35% male)	37%	(65% female/35% male)
Yes	75%	(45% female/55% male)	63%	(41% female/59% male)

Note: N = 516 randomly sampled adults

Khayelitsha report it is appropriate for neighbors to kill a criminal (either accused of theft or murder) demonstrates how widespread the legitimacy of this practice is. While the respondents are not drawn from a representative sample, they were randomly sampled, suggesting that it is likely that these views are common across the township. Table 3.1 reports these breakdowns as well as the gender composition of each cell. Men in South Africa are generally more supportive of lynching than are women; these differences are statistically significant using a difference in means test.

While space and budget limitations prevented us from asking the full battery of questions about governance that we did in Haiti, we look at a few indicators. The linear conditional correlations about approval of lynching in the case of theft and murder are presented in Figure 3.7. Generally speaking, the results are similar (and always in the same direction) for supporting lynching of thieves and of killers. First, respondents reporting a higher level of education are more likely to support lynching, the strongest positive correlation.[77] This suggests that support for lynching may stem from a lack of legitimacy of the justice system, especially among those who are aware it should be functioning more effectively. We do not find a statistically significant association between those who report going to the police for dispute adjudication and support for lynching; this could be evidence of police complicity in lynchings. Those who report more assets are slightly less likely to report supporting lynching; this is strongest and statistically significant for thieves, consistent with a stronger sense of confidence and security in state enforcement of contracts and property rights.

Those who report assessing their local councilors (the most common local level government leader) as performing their duties well are less likely

---

[77] While this correlation is strong, our sample does not have significant variation in education; more than half of the sample reports having completed high school. As a result, we are cautious about relying on this result for future theory building.

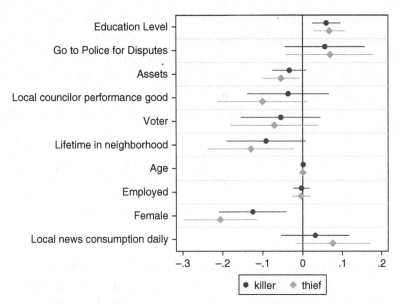

Figure 3.7 Correlates of Lynching Approval in Khayelitsha Township

to support lynching for thieves (the relationship for killers is not statistically significant). As before, confidence in a well-performing government seems to reduce lynching support, consistent with our theory. We find no significant association between support of lynching and reporting of voting in the most recent elections. Self-reported turnout rates are quite high, potentially creating difficulty detecting changes in behavior. Those who report having lived in the neighborhood their entire lives are less likely to support lynching. While we are unable to test explanations directly, one plausible reason for this finding is that lifelong community members may feel uncomfortable with the swiftness of lynching as a form of justice for someone they might know well. We see no effect for age of respondent or employment status. As noted above, women in South Africa are less likely to support lynching. Finally, those who consume local news daily are more likely to support lynching (though the relationship is not statistically significant).

In sum, our data from Khayelitsha confirm high levels of support for lynching. What is remarkable about the South African case is that the state has sophisticated judicial institutions, and in theory, state capacity is quite high. Gang violence and gang governance are not common in the same way they are in Haiti. However, the history of apartheid and the emergence and acceptance of practices of protest and resistance – particularly from the ANC – has had lasting effects in some townships, both in terms of a lack of trust in the state and familiarity with locally administered punishment. This pattern suggests that, despite a broadly functioning judicial system on the national level, there can remain pockets of the state where lynching is sustained due to "cynicism about the police, mistrust of the courts and a belief that mob justice is the only form of effective justice in a corrupt system."[78] In order to carefully explore our theory, we turn to more detailed analysis of lynching using local data from Port-au-Prince, Haiti, in Section 4.

4 Local Governance, Legitimacy, and Lynching in Port-au-Prince

"But most of the time, you know how it goes in Haiti, the population will take care of that person."

–Focus group participant, Port-au-Prince[79]

Haiti provides a vital setting to understand how governance is linked to legitimacy and support for lynching. In this section, we leverage observational, focus group, and survey data from Port-au-Prince to test the hypotheses and assess the observable implications described in Section 2.

First, we show that when the state is viewed as providing effective governance, respondents rate its legitimacy as high and gang legitimacy as low. Those who assess the state as legitimate also strongly disapprove of lynching. Second, we find that state repression – in the form of political violence and police abuse – degrades the state's legitimacy, but does not consistently increase gang legitimacy. However, poor state legitimacy increases support for lynching as a practice. Finally, we find that service provision by gangs increases assessments of gang legitimacy, but does not consistently diminish state legitimacy. Those who assess gangs as legitimate, however, are also more likely to approve of lynching. These results confirm our hypotheses and illustrate the complex linkages between governance, perceptions of legitimacy, and lynching approval.

4.1 Background and Case Selection

Port-au-Prince is an excellent case to understand the effects of governance because of the wide variety of actors on the ground that provide governance and services to the population. In addition to the Haitian state and its agents (the Haitian National Police, or HNP),[80] the UN has had a stabilization mission and

---

[78] "Vigilante Killings on the 'Field of Death' in South African Township," www.theglobeandmail.com /news/world/vigilante-killings-on-the-field-of-death-in-south-african-township/article17052460/.

[79] Focus Group 2, Port-au-Prince, May 15, 2017.

[80] Haiti lacked a military of its own between 1995 and 2017, during which the HNP were the only state agents with the legitimate use of force.

peacekeeping locally since 2004, numerous INGOs have significant operations, and there are a sizable number of local NGOs and church groups that provide services to the population.

As the site of the first and only successful slave revolution in history, the utility of violence for accomplishing the noble goals of independence and freedom is deeply embedded in Haitian culture. However, the violence of the formation of the Haitian state – beginning from the extreme physical conditions of the pre-revolutionary slave plantations followed by the bloody Haitian Revolution – has also left negative cultural legacies that still shape contemporary norms about violence.[81]

In addition, as the least developed country in the Western hemisphere, with recent periods of civil war,[82] local unrest due to contemporary gang violence, and relatively high rates of lynching, Haiti presents a critical case. Although we do not claim that Haiti is representative of the Global South or of the dynamics of governance elsewhere, it is a useful case from which to build insights that could be applied to a variety of contexts. Despite Haiti's somewhat unique history, the dynamics of its politics are broadly generalizable to other contexts with weak or absent governments.[83]

Port-au-Prince is the capital city, with many local gangs that operate throughout urban areas. Criminal gangs govern broad swaths of the slums, or "popular zones" there.[84] Though they have no explicitly political aims, gangs provide a practical challenge to the Haitian state's authority by controlling territory as well as providing basic goods and services to the local population. Gang governance in this context demonstrates that complex systems of governance – including violent governance – can arise even absent explicit goals and efforts to replace the state.

As in many highly unequal societies, particularly with an ineffective or untrusted security sector, the state may work best for those in the middle. The very wealthy bypass the state, paying for private security (Édouard and Dandoy 2016), while the poorest are often outside the reach of the

---

[81] On the Haitian Revolution, see Dubois (2005). On cultural legacies of violence, see, for example, Fatton (2007) and Willman and Marcelin (2010).

[82] Social scientists consider the period of civil war in Haiti to have occurred between 1991 and 1995 (e.g., Fearon and Laitin 2003).

[83] See Kivland (2020: 13), who presents a cogent argument against the idea that Haiti is an exceptional case, or "an aberrant, odd country."

[84] "Gangs" are challenging to define and measure; we will discuss our measurement choices and ethical considerations. For a richly detailed critique of why "gangs" is an inappropriate description of the armed community-based organizations known as *baz*, see Kivland (2020: Introduction, 1–29).

state and must turn to illicit organizations or self-policing. One focus group participant joked that gangs have supplanted the state in terms of security in his neighborhood and gang surveillance even goes by the nickname, "le police."[85] While rural areas have less police presence than urban regions and are also skeptical of police,[86] the urban areas we study are deeply distrustful of the police.

4.1.1 Lynching in Historical Context

Lynching has long been a part of Haitian conceptions of justice, and there are documented reports of lynching as early as the nineteenth century.[87] For nearly three decades (1957–1986), Presidents François and Jean-Claude Duvalier notoriously engaged in severe forms of repression of the Haitian population, largely through the use of a militia officially called the *Volontaires de la sécurité nationale* (VSN), commonly referred to as *Tontons Macoutes,* and the secret police, the *Service Détectif.* Among the various forms of extreme repression common during the reign of the Duvaliers were torture, summary executions, and holding prisoners without charge. The result was the virtual disappearance of political opponents, labor unions, student activists, and an independent press. Some scholars argue that this period led to a normalization of violent control of the population; however, lynching during this period was rare (e.g., D'Adesky 1991).

After the fall of Jean-Claude ("Baby Doc") Duvalier in 1986, the incidence of lynching spiked. Beginning in 1986, lynching was used against supporters and sympathizers of Duvalier (and those suspected thereof), especially members of the reviled Tontons Macoutes (D'Adesky 1991). Lynching victims included voodoo priests and priestess suspected of being supporters of Duvalier. Lynching again was commonly reported during Jean-Bertrand Aristide's first term as president in 1991. In particular, the practice in which tires are forced over a victim's shoulders and then set on fire, called "necklacing" – or *supplice du Père Lebrun* (literally, the torture of Father Lebrun, the name of a local tire dealer) – became a frequent form of violence in this period, and an increasingly important tool in the contentious politics of Haiti. Some argue that Aristide

---

[85] Focus Group 2, Port-au-Prince, Haiti, May 15, 2017.

[86] Schwartz (2008: 22) notes, "In general, the people, especially people in the rural areas, saw [the police] as outsiders who caused more problems than they solved and who were totally unreliable in the case of crime, indeed, inclined to save the criminal and persecute the victims."

[87] This section draws on MINUSTAH (2017), the only UN report on the phenomenon of lynching in Haiti.

implicitly encouraged mob violence, due to public statements such as, "Without a system of justice that is not corrupt, the people must remain vigilant" (D'Adesky 1991).

More recent spates of lynching have been linked to periods of unrest or anxiety, such as lynching of voodoo priests following the 2010 cholera outbreak[88]; media reports include at least sixty-eight victims of cholera-related lynching by late 2010. Beyond these extraordinary episodes, lynching has generally increased as insecurity increased, especially among the city's most vulnerable residents. In addition to perceptions of impunity and corruption (compounded by low pay for law enforcement), justice seems utterly inaccessible to many Haitians, for several reasons: the fact that the language of the justice system is French (which many Creole-speaking Haitians neither speak nor understand), "archaic" laws, and the numerous fees, costs, and bribes associated with pursuing a case (INURED 2017: 20, 22). As Édouard and Dandoy (2016: 7) explain, many residents are increasingly facing "an awareness that people were left on their own and no one was protecting them." As a result, community responses to violence reflect "public exasperation with recurring robberies, rapes and murder, usually in marginal neighborhoods" (Édouard and Dandoy 2016: 8).

4.1.2 Vigilantism in Historical Context

While formal, organized vigilante groups, called *brigades* in Haiti, are outside the scope of our analysis (as we discussed in Section 2), some brigades are reported to commit lynchings, and the historical growth of vigilante groups follows a similar path to less organized forms of collective violence. In one study of vigilantism in Haiti, a report prepared for Oxfam by Édouard and Dandoy (2016), the authors describe the sense of insecurity in Haiti, especially in the slum areas, as "off the scale" due to factors such as poverty, changes in cultural values, overcrowding, and the availability of weapons.

Brigades have changed dramatically over time (Édouard and Dandoy 2016). Earlier brigades were inspired by Marxist ideology, and typically viewed the state as repressive. Many of these early groups offered social services, including emergency first-responder services. Some brigades were formed explicitly to

---

[88] Voodoo priests are both revered and feared, making them targets when seemingly inexplicable events occur. Nick Allen, "A dozen killed in Haiti cholera witch-hunt," *The Telegraph*, December 3, 2010: www.telegraph.co.uk/news/worldnews/centralamericaandthecaribbean/haiti/8180242/A-dozen-killed-in-Haiti-cholera-witch-hunt.html.

protect against the state itself. For example, following the collapse of the dictatorship in 1986, brigades emerged in poorer neighborhoods to protect residents from the notorious Tonton Macoutes. Similarly, the disbanding of the Haitian armed forces in 1995 caused increased distrust and a fear of corruption in state security and justice institutions.

Contemporary brigades are distinct from the earlier incarnations, viewing the state as the preferred authority, and the brigades as a means of filling in where the police are falling short. Many contemporary brigades are formal, and service in such a group is a respected position in the community. Often brigades have the tacit approval of the local police, and conduct surveillance, question subjects, and mete out punishments, including lynchings. In return, community members provide support in the form of food and payments. Moreover, as Édouard and Dandoy (2016: 34) write about vigilante groups in Haiti, "Brigades defy government authority but do not challenge the principle of the state itself."

While we do not study brigades – in part because they are sometimes seen as an extension of the state rather than a challenger – it can be difficult to analyze brigades as separate from gangs and unorganized community groups, and the observational data can be murky. Even with first-hand reports from witnesses, it would be nearly impossible to measure with certainty which lynching events were truly spontaneous and which were perceived as spontaneous, but actually orchestrated by a brigade. In addition, it is unlikely that brigade-perpetrated lynching would be reported to the authorities, making data based on police reports particularly problematic for capturing brigade lynching. To address some of these concerns, our survey measures are designed to explicitly identify neighbors and community members, rather than brigades, as the perpetrators of lynching.

4.1.3 Background on Gangs in Haiti

While a full accounting of the history of gangs in Haiti is too complex to detail here, we provide some basic background information to orient the reader.[89] The presence of nonstate armed groups has long peppered Haiti's tumultuous history, including the feared Tonton Macoutes during the Duvalier dictatorships and the infamous *chimères* of the Aristide era. Some sources trace the contemporary rise of violent neighborhood gangs in Haiti to Aristide's provision of weapons to local groups called *baz* in exchange for their political support of his regime (Becker 2010). While gangs are often violent, they also provide social

---

[89] For further information on gangs and other armed nonstate actors in Haiti, see Kolbe (2013).

services, as we will document. The reason for providing these services, besides income generation, is to enable gangs to "expand ... their sphere of influence within their neighborhoods" (INURED 2017: 30). Kivland (2020: 5) describes the broad range of social and political activities that baz undertake, including "to protect members' wellbeing, furnish their social needs and benefits, and advocate for their upward mobility." Kivland argues that to call baz "gangs" fails to capture the true nature of the baz, a "part-social clique, part-band, part-political association, part-development organization."

More generally, there is a long-term and intertwined relationship between the various types of armed groups in Haiti – including gangs, local militias, and private security organizations – that is "rooted in Haiti's winner-take-all politics," (Berg 2010) wherein political leaders use armed groups to gain and maintain power. The political goals of these groups shift over time; some are organized by political leaders or wealthy families of the business elite, while others are more grassroots local militias, who are then armed by political leaders from all sides. Because of these complex political relationships, the gangs in Haiti are arguably more analogous to rebel groups in other contexts than to typical criminal street gangs.[90]

The collusion between the elite and gangs is widely recognized. Two scholars of gangs noted in an op-ed, "As everyone in Haiti knows, ... specific politicians, business leaders and wealthy landowners serve as the gangs' chief patrons."[91] These patrons "back some individuals and provide them with financial support and guns to become area gang leaders."[92] In a session of the Senate, during which a police chief was testifying regarding arms trafficking, a senator declared to his colleagues, "We all have our gangs."[93] Gangs require the support of these patrons for resources and arms; common weapons include knives, machetes, and small firearms (INURED 2017: 32). As one local saying goes, "Guns are cheap; ammunition is expensive"[94]; patrons provide the ammunition.

Beyond support from the elite, sources of gang income vary. Some gangs raise funds through organized crime, including kidnapping and drug smuggling. Groups also use extortion, collecting money from local shops to offer protection

---

[90] Kivland (2020: 14) likens the baz in Haiti to civil defense groups in West Africa, for example.

[91] Athena Kolbe and Robert Muggah, 2013, "Haiti's 'Gangs' Can Be a Force for Good," *Ottawa Citizen,* June 11, A12.

[92] "The Events in La Saline: From Power Struggle between Armed Gangs to State-Sanctioned Massacre," National Network for the Defense of Human Rights, December 1, 2018: http://rnddh .org/content/uploads/2018/12/10-Rap-La-Saline-1Dec2018-Ang1.pdf.

[93] That senator has since retracted his statement, but it remains a remarkable admission in an open session of the Senate. Author interview with Jacqueline Charles, July 31, 2019.

[94] Author interview with Jacqueline Charles, July 31, 2019.

from rival groups and to avoid road closures that would prevent the flow of customers to businesses or market centers.[95]

Estimating the prevalence of gangs is difficult and it is unclear if the number of gangs or their membership has increased over time. Nonetheless, gang activity is most apparent in the slum areas of the city, particularly in neighborhoods of Martissant and Port-au-Prince (INURED 2017). While Cité Soleil is one of the most notorious bases for gangs historically, *Miami Herald* journalist Jacqueline Charles noted there was an apparent calm in Cité Soleil in mid-2019.[96] In addition, there are signs that gang activity and recruitment have started shifting to more rural areas of the country, due to deteriorating social conditions and increasing poverty, and possibly also the spread of social media. Several sources report that gang violence seems to increase during elections, another indication of collusion with politicians and aspiring political leaders.

There has been a recent resurgence of gang violence, including the worst massacre in a decade that occurred in November 2018: a two-day episode of extraordinary violence in the La Saline neighborhood of Port-au-Prince, in which fighting between five rival gangs resulted in a large number of deaths. A UN report estimated the number of deaths at twenty-six people, with twelve still missing (MINUJUSTH 2019), but other sources report much higher numbers.[97] Beyond the murders, which appear to be largely indiscriminate, the bodies of the dead were fed to pigs, and there were reports of the lynching of a ten-month-old baby, and several public gang rapes.[98] UN investigators issued a report that condemned the police for not intervening during the attack, and noted that some of the perpetrators wore police uniforms and that two government officials were present at the massacre.[99] Whether this massacre was an anomaly or a harbinger of a new era of extreme violence remains to be seen; the uncertainty is heightened because the UN peacekeeping mission left in October 2019 during a period of heightened insecurity.

---

[95] Jacqueline Charles, "Dozens Brutally Killed, Raped in Haiti Massacre: Police Say. 'Even Young Children Were Not Spared,'" *Miami Herald*, May 15, 2019: www.miamiherald.com/news/nation-world/world/americas/haiti/article230380739.html.

[96] Author interview with Jacqueline Charles, July 31, 2019.

[97] The National Network for the Defense of Human Rights reports fifty-nine deaths; the report lists the names and ages of all victims, which includes several young children. http://rnddh.org/content/uploads/2018/12/10-Rap-La-Saline-1Dec2018-Ang1.pdf.

[98] La Saline is the site of the largest outdoor market in the city, and the violence occurred between two periods of massive protests and demonstrations against the current administration. La Saline is a pro-opposition area, which may be why it was targeted for violence. Author interview with Jacqueline Charles, July 31, 2019. See also: www.miamiherald.com/news/nation-world/world/americas/haiti/article230380739.html.

[99] Jacqueline Charles, "U.N. Investigators Say Haitian Government Condoned Massacre that Left Dozens Dead," *Miami Herald*, June 21, 2019: www.miamiherald.com/news/nation-world/world/americas/haiti/article231826588.html

4.2 Data Sources

4.2.1 Focus Groups

To collect primary data about gangs, gang governance, the state, and lynching, we conducted a series of eight focus groups with 48 Haitian adults in May 2017 and September 2019.[100] Participants were recruited from across the "popular zones" in Port-au-Prince. Each participant was compensated for their time and provided with transportation, funding, and a meal. Professional facilitators led the groups, and each group was simultaneously translated from Haitian Creole to English for the authors' comprehension. The authors then took notes of the discussions.

4.2.2 Measures of Attitudes about Lynching

We created and fielded an original household survey in Port-au-Prince, including in gang-governed areas, to study variation in the perceptions and attitudes about security, the state, local gangs, and service provision. Our goal was to use respondents' answers to our survey questions to illustrate dynamics in the micro-foundations of governance, sovereignty, and legitimacy.[101] We fielded the survey with an embedded experiment (described later in this section) of 1,066 adults in Port-au-Prince in July 2017. We will discuss sampling and data collection, as well as the specific measures we use, in more detail. We also address ethical concerns related to some of the sensitive questions we posed and how we mitigated risk later in the section.

4.2.3 Reports of Lynching

To explore patterns of lynching in Port-au-Prince, we draw on a remarkable data source containing descriptions of incidents of fatalities documented by a local NGO. Beginning in 2002, *Komisyon Episkopal Nasyonal Jistis ak Lapè* (JILAP), or The National Episcopal Commission for Justice and Peace, has collected detailed information about lethal violence in the greater Port-au-Prince metropolitan area using designated reporters in each major area of the city. In addition to consulting with these observers in neighborhoods around Port-au-Prince, representatives from JILAP also meet with witnesses and/or independently investigate reported deaths. Finally, they supplement the reports

---

[100] Details about focus groups, including the participants and recruitment process, are in the Online Appendix.

[101] As we argued in Section 1, these dynamics have been largely overlooked in previous political science research, which has focused almost exclusively on the dynamics associated with armed conflict, in which actors seek to revise the boundaries and authority of the state.

they collect with information gathered from newspapers in order to provide a comprehensive picture of victims of lethal violence. One of JILAP's goals is to make transparent the incidence of killings and accidents in Port-au-Prince; official crime data are not otherwise made public.[102] As the director of JILAP stated in an interview, "The purpose of our project is to make the state aware of what is going on in order to avoid the situation of too much violence, or the state ignoring dead bodies on the streets."[103]

JILAP issues a quarterly narrative report in Haitian Creole that provides information about incidents of lethal violence. The reported deaths include homicides, as well as numerous other causes of death, such as suicides, deaths due to traffic accidents, and – our main category of interest – lynching. We consolidated, translated, and coded more than 10,000 reported deaths between 2002 and 2017 to create a measure of the number of fatalities recorded per month.[104] From this universe of cases, we isolated the 405 deaths that were reported to be due to lynching in the description. We then coded each lynching description for details about the method of execution, the actors involved, and precipitating reason for the attack. These 405 incidents of lynching between 2002 and 2017 provide the basis for the analysis that follows in this section. While we should use caution about generalizing from a sample drawn from one source from a single city, the patterns and descriptions about these 405 incidents are both striking and informative.[105]

4.3 Patterns of Lynching in Port-au-Prince

Using the JILAP data, we describe several patterns of lynching in Port-au-Prince, including the victims, method of execution, and precipitating cause (that is, the alleged crime that sparked lynching as a reprisal).[106] There has been only one in-depth report about lynchings and attempted lynchings in Haiti, based on

---

[102] Official HNP/UN crime data are not publicly available at the necessary levels of disaggregation, and many months of the authors' attempts at accessing disaggregated crime statistics from the UN and the HNP were unsuccessful. Nonetheless, the JILAP data, which we use as our primary source, appear to be less biased and more detailed. For instance, we were granted access by a confidential source to a small subset of official UN data on lethal violence in 2015–2016. These data, however, show little to no violence in areas of the city (e.g., Cité Soleil) commonly recognized to be among the most violent at the time. Because the JILAP data, on the other hand, contain many reports of homicide in the areas most widely recognized to be violent, we rely solely on the JILAP data in this analysis.

[103] Interview with Jocelyne Colas Noël, JILAP, Port-au-Prince, March 9, 2017.

[104] These data are publicly available on Harvard Dataverse (Cohen and Jung 2018): https://doi.org /10.7910/DVN/KX5JRF.

[105] As we note later, the lynching patterns highlighted in the 405 cases from JILAP are fairly consistent with those described by the MINUSTAH report, the only other available data source (see the Online Appendix).

[106] While the data source we use is quite rich, these patterns should be interpreted with caution because of missing information in each case, as noted. Summary statistics are reported in Table A.4 in the Online Appendix.

incidents reported to police, published by the Human Rights Section of MINUSTAH and the Office of the High Commissioner United Nations Human Rights Commission in January 2017. The report, which describes the only other existing quantitative data source, finds that lynching is widespread and occurs with impunity. We use the MINUSTAH (2017) report as a source to compare the patterns we uncover in the JILAP data.[107] Despite many attempts, we were unable to gain access to these police report-based data directly.

The MINUSTAH data indicate that the Oueste Department (which contains Port-au-Prince and its surrounding areas) is in the area of the country that experiences the most lynchings, by approximately four times, suggesting that the JILAP data covers the region where lynchings are most likely to occur. In the Online Appendix, we compare the basic patterns in these two data sources, and discuss the potential biases in both datasets. The JILAP data and the MINUSTAH report contain similar patterns with respect to the victims of lynching being overwhelmingly men, and the most common precipitating crime being theft or property crime.

4.3.1 Victims

A striking pattern consistent with the cross-national data is that those killed via lynching are overwhelmingly men. Of those cases for which we have data on gender, 97 percent of those who were killed by lynching were men.[108] However, the gender of the victim is noted in only a minority of the JILAP source documents.[109] One possible reason for the disproportionate number of male victims may be that young men comprise the majority of perpetrators (and victims) of most acts of violent crime around the world (Gibbons 2013; Ormhaug et al. 2009). Given that lynching is a response to crime, we would expect that most people targeted for lynching would be young men. An exception, as we discussed in Section 3, is that women are more likely to be accused of sorcery, making women overrepresented among lynching victims that were precipitated by suspicion of witchcraft.

4.3.2 Methods of Execution

We next turn to the method of execution, displayed in Figure 4.1. We coded any description about the method and process; 79 percent of lynching descriptions

---

[107] In addition to the data collection process and time periods differing slightly, the MINUSTAH data include reports of *attempted* lynchings as well as lynchings from the entire country. The JILAP data do not include attempted lynchings (all JILAP observations resulted in an actual body) and only were collected in the Oueste Department, which includes Port-au-Prince.

[108] See Figure A.3 in the Online Appendix for a breakdown of victim gender (when reported).

[109] Only 25 percent of cases of lynching have sufficient information for us to establish the gender of those killed by lynching. However, the MINUSTAH (2017) data also suggest that the vast majority of victims in Haiti are men.

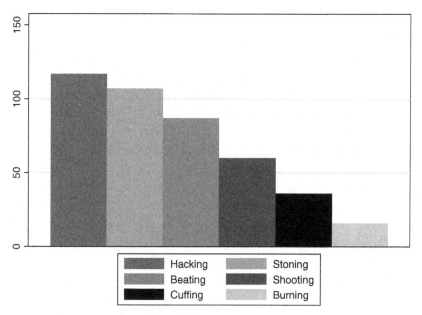

Figure 4.1 Method of Lynching in Port-au-Prince

Note: N=320 cases where method was reported; *Source*: JILAP dataset, Cohen and Jung (2018)

contained information about the method(s) of execution. Note that these categories are not mutually exclusive; for example, the victim may be beaten and subsequently burned.

Figure 4.1 highlights that the four most common methods for killing via lynching are stoning, hacking (stabbing), beating, and "cuffing" (restraining and then beating and/or burning the victim.) As discussed previously, these are all forms of group violence that require numerous participants.

4.3.3 Precipitating Cause

While only about 60 percent of the descriptions of lynching make note about the precipitating crime, of those that do, the overwhelming majority appear to be property crimes.[110] This is consistent with observations made by experts and our focus group participants, as well as the MINUSTAH (2017) report on the topic. This evidence is also in line with the significant proportion of lynchings attributed to property crimes in the cross-national data described in Section 3. In sum, this

---

[110] In the descriptions compiled by JILAP, "theft" generally describes a property crime, while any entry mentioning murder or rape is coded as a crime against a person. See Figure A.4 in the Online Appendix for a breakdown of precipitating crimes.

Table 4.1 Public Support for Lynching in Port-au-Prince

	Approve of lynching vs. state justice system		Approve of lynching of murderers		Approve of lynching of thieves	
Yes	24%	(51% women/ 49% men)	44%	(54% women/ 46% men)	49%	(60% women/ 40% men)
No	76%	(49% women/ 51% men)	56%	(46% women/ 54% men)	51%	(40% women/ 60% men)

Note: While we ask these three questions on the survey, we show the responses to general approval and lynching of thieves in the statistical analysis (that is, we do not use the murder measure); these represent the two measures that uncovered the lowest and highest approval of lynching, respectively.

evidence points to instances where lynchings were precipitated by crimes other than rape, kidnapping, or murder. While it might be assumed that punishment by death would be reserved for particularly heinous crimes, we find evidence that this is not the case in Port-au-Prince, where 44 percent of respondents report approving lynching those accused of murder, compared to 49 percent of respondents who report approving lynching of thieves (see Table 4.1).[111]

4.4 Survey Data

We now turn to describing our survey data collection process and the survey measures that form the core of the remainder of this section, where we test our central theory. We first describe our sampling and data collection process, then discuss our indicators of support for lynching, followed by our measures of legitimacy and governance in Haiti.[112] The administrative structure of the Haitian state is organized in the following manner: the state is comprised of 10 departments; departments are subdivided into 42 arrondissements, and arrondissements are subdivided into 144 communes. As described in the next section, our sampling was at the commune level in the Oueste Department in the Port-au-Prince arrondissement.

---

[111] This pattern could be due to more nuance than our closed-choice question was able to capture ("Now imagine your neighbors caught a killer in your neighborhood, who are murdered one of your neighbors. The neighbors caught him and then killed the person as a punishment. Is this appropriate?" [*Yes, Depends, No, Refuse to answer*]). For example, respondents may believe that the victim's family has the primary right to punish the offender rather than the neighborhood. Our measures only allow us to gauge support for lynching (collective violence) relative to state mechanisms rather than revenge-motivated violence.

[112] Summary statistics are reported in Table A.5 in the Online Appendix.

4.4.1 Survey Sampling Strategy

Creating a sampling frame proved challenging. Because of the lack of a recent census – the most recent census data are from 2003, prior to the 2010 earthquake that caused massive death and displacement – there exists no method to assess accurately the representativeness of the data.[113] Instead, we prioritized sampling of areas with exposure to violence rather than of representativeness in order to be able to control for relative exposure to lethal violence.[114] Levels of lethal violence due to crime, gangs, and the police are high in some neighborhoods.[115] By sampling on prior exposure to violence at the commune level (our best measure of violence exposure), we ensure that there are sufficient respondents in each commune with high exposure to violence. However, even in communes with relatively high levels of violence, there is significant diversity of actual exposure – meaning there are many relatively "safe" areas even in the communes that are generally violent.

We contracted a local Haitian survey firm, to administer our survey. We sampled respondents from six of the eight communes in the Port-au-Prince arrondissement.[116] We apportioned clusters of twelve respondents to communes according to exposure to recent episodes of lethal violence; specifically, the probability proportional to the incidence of lethal violence in the previous two years (2015–2016). Within communes, we identified the universe of potential clusters by laying a 250m by 250m grid over a commune map, and removing obviously inaccessible clusters (e.g., in a ravine, on a mountain, or in the ocean), as well as those that the implementing partner deemed logistically infeasible (e.g., too sparsely populated or populated only with businesses, not households).[117] From that universe of eligible clusters, we randomly selected a number of clusters proportionate to the commune-level exposure to lethal violence. Within each cluster, households were selected based on a random walk by each enumerator. Within each household, the enumerator selected the adult of the same gender who had the most recent

---

[113] See also Gordon and Young (2017), who faced similar sampling challenges in their survey study in metropolitan Port-au-Prince.

[114] We also collected data for several other projects that rely on measuring exposure to violence.

[115] Based on the data compiled from JILAP, homicides due to gang violence more than reached the equivalent of a low-intensity conflict (at least twenty-five deaths) on an annual basis between 2002 and 2016 (Cohen and Jung 2018).

[116] The sample includes all major population areas in the capital city. We excluded two communes (Kenscoff and Gressier) that are more sparsely populated and farther from the city center for both budgetary and logistical reasons. The six sampled communes include those most likely to have gang governance.

[117] Our implementing partner preferred to work from "crosshairs" rather than within grid-squares, restricting distance from the starting point to 125m to ensure no overlap with another cluster even should the neighboring "crosshair" be selected.

birthday. Enumerator teams were comprised of equal numbers of men and women, ensuring gender balance within the sample.

4.4.2 Assessing the Presence of "Gangs": Measurement and Ethics

Gangs in Port-au-Prince are difficult to measure using survey methods. First, gangs go by a variety of names, and there is some interchangeability of terms in common parlance. In Haitian Creole, *baz* means "base," and roughly translates to team; *bandi*, meaning bandit, refers to a violent criminal group; and *brigade* is a local vigilante/self-defense group. All three terms are used to describe types of extralegal local armed organizations that operate on the neighborhood level in Port-au-Prince. In our survey, we asked respondents about all three types of groups: baz, bandi, and brigades. While it would have been ideal to analyze separately the information we collected on each of the types of armed actors, we faced significant measurement challenges due to definitional issues. In our pre-testing phase, we found surprisingly little consensus over the specific terms for the various armed actors and were unable to reliably measure each group separately. Because the specific definitions for similar groups vary from neighborhood to neighborhood – or even from person to person – we aggregate all of these groups into the single, simplified category of "gangs" in the following analyses.[118] One discussion that emerged in focus groups was that a gang might be called a *baz* (a more positive term) in one's own neighborhood but a gang (a decidedly derogatory term) in a rival neighborhood. Survey data show there is little difference in how these groups are perceived. As a result, in the proceeding analyses, we pool across these three sub-types. We acknowledge that this aggregation fails to capture some differences between these groups. In addition, while aggregating these groups is useful for some analyses, it prevents us from testing other hypotheses, such as whether there is less frequent spontaneous vigilantism where brigades are effective at punishing crime.[119]

Beyond measurement, we also faced significant ethical considerations designing a survey instrument that elicited opinions about gangs, especially in gang-controlled areas. We employed several mitigation strategies to reduce risk to our team and to respondents, and to increase the veracity of responses. First,

---

[118] Kivland (2020: 22–23) notes that one of her research subjects, Frantzy, was an active member of a baz in the Bel Air neighborhood. Frantzy both self-identified as a *bandi* in one anecdote (when he was presenting himself as a bodyguard for Kivland), and feared being called a bandi by others in his workplace. These incidents show how the label of bandi is socially constructed, and demonstrates how fluid the notion of who qualifies as a bandi can be, even among the members of the organizations themselves.

[119] Kolbe and Muggah (2013) make a similar point in their op-ed; they argue that foreigners tend to oversimplify a vast array of armed groups into the one general category of "gangs." However, as we explain, we found this oversimplification to be unavoidable.

the Haitian survey firm employed enumerators from the specific neighborhoods where the survey was to be fielded. Based on previous experience, they felt this was especially prudent in gang-controlled areas, where any outsider – even a local person from a different neighborhood – would be regarded with immediate suspicion, and potentially prevented from fielding the survey – or worse, may be harassed or even beaten by gang members.

Second, in pre-testing the survey, the enumerators expressed concern that the survey instrument on their tablets contained questions about gangs (bandi). Enumerators felt that were a gang member to ask to review the survey (not uncommon, in their prior experience), the enumerators might be made unsafe if the instrument included questions about bandi in particular.[120] Together, we innovated a solution: while the enumerator would verbally ask respondents about all three terms for gangs, including bandi, the text in the survey instrument would read only *mét*, Haitian Creole for "chief," a generic term similar to "dude" or "guy." Our training thus included saying aloud the word bandi to the respondent whenever the word mét appeared in the text of the survey instrument.

Finally, we asked respondents to share whether there were gangs operating in their neighborhoods. To determine the extent of underreporting, we also asked the enumerator to report seeing a visible gang presence based on their own perception at the survey site. To decrease reporting bias, we sought to destigmatize relationships with gangs through using normalizing language in the preamble to the questions (e.g., "In some places, baz help people in the neighborhoods. For example, there are those that pay for school, and those that give people access to water, electricity, or food aid. Are baz around here that do that for this neighborhood?").

4.4.3 Survey Measures of Lynching Approval

While we did not ask directly about individual participation in lynching, to gauge support for lynching, we asked respondents a series of questions regarding their opinions on the practice of lynching versus state institutions:

• **General Preference for Lynching Over State Justice**: "Do you prefer lynching [neighborhood justice] or turning criminals over to the justice system?" [*Criminals should always be turned over to the justice system; Sometimes criminals should be turned over to the police, and sometimes neighborhood justice should deal with criminals; Neighborhood justice should always deal with criminals*]

---

[120] Enumerators reported that they felt comfortable verbally asking respondents about bandi; their concern was limited to the written text of the survey.

Respondents were coded as approving of lynching if they responded that they preferred lynching sometimes or always.

• **Approval of Lynching for Property Crimes**: "Imagine your neighbors caught a thief in your neighborhood. The thief broke into a home, and stole something. Your neighbors then caught and killed the thief as a punishment. Is this appropriate?" [*Yes; Depends; No*]

Respondents were coded as approving lynching for property crimes if they responded yes or depends.

• **Approval of Lynching for Murder**: "Now imagine your neighbors caught a killer in your neighborhood who murdered one of your neighbors. The neighbors caught him and then killed the person as a punishment. Is this appropriate?" [*Yes; Depends; No*]

Respondents were coded as approving lynching for murder if they responded yes or depends.[121]

While our findings (displayed in Table 4.1) suggest that general approval for lynching is low (25 percent), the questions about the appropriateness of lynching in response to particular crimes revealed widespread support.[122] Of respondents, 49 percent believe it is appropriate for neighbors to kill a thief, while 44 percent believe it is appropriate for neighbors to kill a murderer. Additionally, we find that women, who likely feel more vulnerable to theft, are more likely than men to support lynching in the case of property crimes (60 percent vs. 40 percent support among men; notably, women and men are equally likely to support lynching in the case of murder.)

Context is important in making sense of these responses: our respondents are residents in some of the poorest areas of Port-au-Prince and theft of property is viewed as fundamentally threatening to the victims' basic survival; as a result, the violence of the act of petty theft is more severe than may be initially assumed.[123] Our focus group data add additional nuance to the survey responses. In response to a hypothetical question about the appropriateness of killing a suspected thief who was caught in his neighborhood, one man noted, "If this happened in my

---

[121] The survey questions for property crime and murder presume guilt, although in reality there can often be significant uncertainty over whether the person being punished is actually the perpetrator. We were concerned that presenting information about a "suspected" criminal would conflate the crime with the judgment of the perpetrator. We instead chose to test a direct measure of an unambiguously guilty perpetrator to get a sense of respondents' views of the appropriate responses when guilt is not in question.

[122] As we show in Section 3, we asked a similar question in South Africa with more extreme results: 63 percent of respondents approved of lynching for thieves and 75 percent for killers.

[123] That slightly more respondents favor lynching for thieves may indicate a belief that the family of a victim, rather than neighbors, have the first right to punish the offender; however, we do not explore this directly.

neighborhood, I would say that the neighbors have done something good. [The lynching] was for all of us. We do not need to tolerate thieves. Once a thief steals, he needs to be punished. This is good justice."[124] When asked how their neighbors might feel after a lynching of a suspected criminal took place in their neighborhood, another added, "If I killed someone in my community who had killed someone, the population would feel happy because the lynching was for the whole community, not just for myself. Instead of being angry, they should tell me, 'My friend, I congratulate you.'"[125]

4.4.4 Survey Measures of Governance Output and Perceptions of Legitimacy

Legitimacy is a notoriously nebulous concept. Surveys offer advantages in operationalizing legitimacy, in that they focus on measuring respondents' perceptions and attitudes. But surveys also have disadvantages, because potential biases in reporting can distort measurement of the underlying concept. In an effort to mitigate these biases and to capture multiple aspects of legitimacy, our survey included several indicators of legitimacy and attitudes about the state, gangs, and other local, national, and international entities providing governance and services in Port-au-Prince. Importantly, we collected measures about state *and* nonstate actors along parallel dimensions.

First, we asked a series of questions about attitudes of indicators of *state support* and *state health*, including attitudes regarding tax collection, whether voting improves state-sponsored services, whether the police make respondents feel safer, and opinions about the reestablishment of the Haitian Army (which was disbanded in 1995 and minimally reinstated in late 2017, a few months after the survey was fielded.) Taken together, these questions suggest a sense of trust in critical functions of the state, including the use and expansion of force, and links of accountability between citizens and government. In line with our conceptions of legitimacy as "rightful rule," each is a measure of how rightful the state is in asking for compliance from citizens.

- **Tax Collection**: "In your opinion, how important is it for the Haitian government to collect taxes from people like you?" [*Very important; Somewhat important; Not so important; Not at all important*]
- **Army Reinstatement**: "Before I begin, I want to remind you Haiti has not had a military since 1995, and right now we just have a small corps of

---

[124] Focus Group 8, Port-au-Prince, September 23, 2019.
[125] Focus Group 8, Port-au-Prince, September 23, 2019.

engineers.[126] Do you think Haiti should expand it to a full army, or should Haiti not have a military again, only the engineers?" [*Haiti should have a full military again; Haiti should not have a full military, only the engineers*]

Second, we inquired about indicators of legitimacy as they pertain to justice and dispute adjudication by both state and nonstate actors. We developed the set of actors in the response list based on feedback from our focus groups, by asking participants to brainstorm all plausible intervenors in interpersonal disputes.

• **Dispute Adjudication by the State and by Gangs**: "If you had a dispute about property with a neighbor, and you could not settle it yourself, who would you turn to in order to settle it? Please tell me all that apply." [*Local elders; Police; MINUSTAH*[127]; *ASEC; CASEC*[128]; *Courts; Religious leader; Gang [Baz; Bandi; Brigade]; Neighbors/friends/family; Local organization; Other*]

Finally, we measure an indicator of gang legitimacy, by asking if, on net, gangs do more good or more harm.

• **Gangs Not Harmful**: "Do gangs [baz/brigades/bandi] do more good for the people in this neighborhood or more harm?" [*Do more good; Do more harm; Do equal amounts of harm and good*]

We code gangs to be a net positive if respondents do not reply "do more harm."

4.4.5 Evidence of Gang Governance

In light of the many development and security problems it is perhaps unsurprising that gangs have emerged in Port-au-Prince, particularly in the post-Aristide era. As we show in Section 3, lynchings were reported prior to the Aristide crises in the early and mid-1990s, and became a more regular occurrence from the 1990s onward.[129] Gangs each control territory in the city and provide extensive governance over them, providing a range of services, an observable output of one form of good governance.

To highlight the diversity of service and governance providers, we conducted a brief census of services, asking respondents whether *any* actor provided to them any of four basic services: road repair, sanitation, water,[130] and

---

[126] The corps of engineers is generally understood to be used for relief and public works efforts only, and is explicitly not a "full army."

[127] MINUSTAH is the acronym for the United Nations Stabilization Mission in Haiti, established on June 1, 2004.

[128] ASEC and CASEC are the local city and sub-city council representatives, respectively.

[129] See the Haiti chart in Figure 3.4.

[130] Only about 8 percent of Haitians can access tap water through the public utility; however, tap water is not potable. As a result, all Haitians must find sources of potable water; the wealthy can purchase bottled water, but the majority of Haitians must use other sources, including (often dirty) rivers and waterways (INURED 2017: 9).

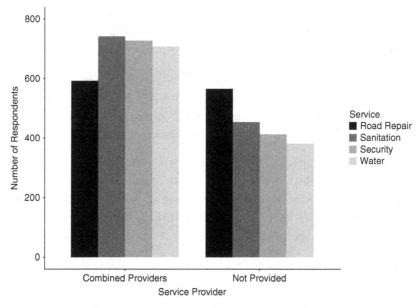

Figure 4.2 Services provided – and not provided – in Port-au-Prince

security.[131] Figure 4.2 highlights three patterns from the services census. First, at least 40 percent of respondents report at least one of the four services are not provided by any actor. This is illustrated by the high frequencies in the right-hand panel. Second, many respondents receive the same service from multiple providers (respondents were able to report services that were provided by multiple groups or actors, so columns can sum to more than our total number of respondents). It is likely that individuals get a single service from multiple actors because the services are insufficiently or irregularly provided; however, we do not have direct survey evidence of this. Finally, only approximately 6 percent of respondents reported receiving all four services from a single provider, and most of these also received duplicate services from other providers.

Next, in Figure 4.3, we look at *which* actors provide each service; respondents could report more than one actor provides any service. Again, a few patterns emerge. First, water services are reported by many respondents to be provided by local NGOs, dwarfing any other reported service by any other provider. Second, local government is the modal provider of road repair. Although infrequently provided, sanitation services are reportedly obtained from gangs, the local government, or

---

[131] These represent major services, but are not an exhaustive list. Kivland (2020), for example, writes about a baz that organized an electricity project in their neighborhood.

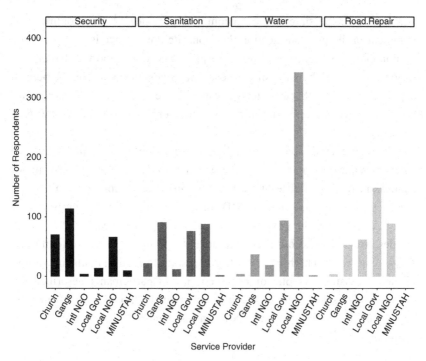

Figure 4.3 Service Provision by Provider Type in Port-au-Prince

a local NGO. Gangs provide all three types of non-security services – sanitation, road repair, and water – in areas they control.

Finally, gangs are the most cited provider of security services, closely followed by the church and local NGOs, though we note that each of these are well under 10 percent of the sample. Few respondents recognize MINUSTAH or the local government as providing security, which may partially reflect residents' generally low opinion of the UN mission or a deep mistrust of police. This patchwork of security providers has led some to call for a more realistic recognition of "the empirical reality of multiple providers of public security" (UN-Habitat quoted in Édouard and Dandoy 2016: 32). But, there is little research that maps these relationships or their consequences on public perceptions of the legitimacy of each provider.

Among the respondents who report receiving all four services from the same actor, several patterns are revealed. First, only 6.3 percent of respondents reported getting all four services from any actor, underscoring the cobbled-together nature of governance for most Haitians. While gangs are a modal service provider as highlighted in Figure 4.3, only 1.7 percent of respondents report gangs provide them with all four services, indicating that they, like the state, are an incomplete provider.[132] This confirms our argument in the previous section that nonstate governance is rarely, if ever, a monopoly. In contrast, among respondents who reported having all services provided by any single actor, *neighbors* account for 73 percent of these cases (n=48 cases total). We will use these 48 cases where *all* basic services are only provided by neighbors as evidence of *self-help governance*.

Taken together, our data paint a picture of incomplete governance by state authorities and by gangs. Expert assessments concur with the patterns in our data. As Jacqueline Charles describes, the slum areas no longer have a strong presence of the UNDP and USAID, or even a large aid agency presence. "Food, clinics, and the government are all absent," Charles said. "The only entities are gangs and ordinary Haitians."[133] In the extreme, we found that respondents rely on highly local self-governance to fill the significant gaps in service provision. As one of our focus group participants described the situation of this self-help approach to governance, "Sometimes it's just the people in the neighborhood. Not an association, just people in the community."[134]

4.5 Testing the Central Theory

We now turn to exploring how legitimacy changes based on receipt of services, and how lynching ultimately emerges. As we argued in Section 2, legitimacy can decay through either state failure or competing governance provision by challengers to the state – in this case, gangs. Our broader empirical strategy follows our theoretical presentation in Section 2. We summarize the strategy and our results below, before turning to a detailed review of the findings.

- First, we analyze the relationship between good state governance and state legitimacy and gang legitimacy, respectively, and then we turn to the relationship between state legitimacy and approval of lynching. We find that respondents who report a well-performing state also perceive the state as strongly legitimate, while perceptions of gang legitimacy are diminished (or at least

---

[132] Only eighteen respondents report getting all of their services from the gangs and none from other actors. Across the entire sample, among the three gang subtypes (baz, bandi, and brigade), baz were clearly the modal provider of all service types, but they were never the only source of any type. All three types of groups were reported to provide each service, with the exception of brigades and water provision. See Table A.6 in the Online Appendix for a breakdown of the four services across the three types of groups.

[133] Author interview with Jacqueline Charles, July 31, 2019.

[134] Focus Group 2, Port-au-Prince, May 15, 2017.

not increased). Finally, we find that state legitimacy is associated with far less approval for lynching (see Table 4.2.)

- Next, we turn to examining if <u>poor state governance</u> is associated with state legitimacy and gang legitimacy, respectively. For completeness, we then again report the relationship between state legitimacy and approval of lynching. We find that respondents who report a poorly performing state also perceive the state as lacking legitimacy; for these respondents, we also find evidence of positive indicators of gang legitimacy. Again, state legitimacy is negatively associated with approval of lynching (see Table 4.3.)

- Third, we investigate the association between <u>good governance by gangs</u> on gang and state legitimacy, respectively. We then analyze whether perceptions of gang legitimacy are associated with increased approval for lynching, and we find that they are (see Table 4.3).

- Finally, we look at the set of cases where <u>community members have turned to self-help governance</u>, and where neither the state nor gangs are providing basic services. Here, we first look at how increasing reliance on neighbors for governance is negatively associated with the legitimacy of both the state and gangs, then how this reliance on neighbors leads to support for lynching (see Table 4.4). Next, we extend the analysis to look at the more extreme case of self-help governance, in which respondents report relying on neighbors for *all* services. In this case, we again look at the effects of self-help governance on state and gang legitimacy and approval of lynching. We find self-help governance is strongly associated with approval of lynching (see Table 4.4).

In the tables that follow, all estimations report coefficients from ordinary least squares regressions, with standard errors clustered at the sampling point. All models include a battery of standard controls (gender, education, age, and religiosity, as proxied by church attendance). Our results are robust to omitting these controls, but we include these to account for possible variation in experience with the state and variation in attitudes about state legitimacy at the individual level.

4.5.1 Good State Governance, Legitimacy, and Lynching

We now turn to analyzing our expectations about good state performance on both state and gang legitimacy, as well as the approval of lynching. In Table 4.2, we use three indicators of the respondent's perceptions of a well-functioning state: whether the respondent has a formal bank account, whether they express confidence in the police, and if they perceive a link between voting and the

Table 4.2 Good State Governance on Legitimacy and Support for Lynching

	State Legitimacy			Gang Legitimacy		Lynching	
	(1)	(2)	(3)	(4)	(5)	(6)	(7)
	Taxes	State Dispute Adjudication	Restore Army	Gang Dispute Adjudication	Gangs Not Harmful	Lynch Approve	Thief Lynch Approve
Formal Bank Account	0.103***	−0.0122	−0.0168	0.0149	0.0478		
	(0.0381)	(0.0637)	(0.0248)	(0.0169)	(0.0408)		
Confidence in Police	0.170***	0.204***	0.0682**	−0.0261*	0.0649		
	(0.0393)	(0.0620)	(0.0263)	(0.0135)	(0.0514)		
Voting Services Link	0.0125	0.125**	−0.0658***	−0.00328	0.0285		
	(0.0355)	(0.0588)	(0.0191)	(0.00993)	(0.0627)		
Taxes Important						−0.0922**	−0.151***
						(0.0362)	(0.0393)
State Dispute Resolution						0.0210	0.0277
						(0.0234)	(0.0258)
Army Restoration						−0.201***	−0.168***
						(0.0626)	(0.0525)

Constant	0.0592***	0.581***	0.845***	0.0895**	0.380***	0.560***	0.746***
	(0.0687)	(0.105)	(0.0475)	(0.0387)	(0.0924)	(0.0773)	(0.0817)
Observations	860	860	826	860	352	847	855
R-squared	0.129	0.098	0.095	0.044	0.413	0.071	0.096
Controls	Yes	Yes	Yes	Yes	Yes	Yes	Yes
FE	Yes	Yes	Yes	Yes	Yes	Yes	Yes

Note: Standard errors clustered at the PSU in parentheses. ***p<0.01, **p<0.05, *p<0.1. All models include commune-level fixed effects. Controls included are: gender, education level, age, and church attendance. Questions not already described in the text were as follows: Respondent indicated they had a formal bank account; Confidence in Police: "When the police are in my neighborhood, I feel safer." [Yes; Depends; No]. Voting Services Link: "In your opinion, does the opportunity to vote in the elections increase the quality of what the government should do for you (like sanitation, electricity, schools, health clinics) in your neighborhood?" [Yes; No].

services provided.[135] In Models 1–3, the dependent variables all capture different aspects of state legitimacy: paying taxes, reporting willingness to rely on the state for dispute adjudication,[136] and support for restoring the Haitian army. In Models 1–3, consistent with Hypothesis 1, which predict perceptions of an actor's effectiveness in governance is positively associated with perceptions of their legitimacy, reports of receiving good governance from the state generally lead to positive assessments of state legitimacy. In particular, there is a strong, positive, and highly statistically significant link between respondents who express confidence in the main instrument of force of the state, the Haitian National Police (HNP), and positive assessments of all aspects of state legitimacy. For example, those who have confidence in the HNP, are 20.4 percentage points more likely to report going to a state agent for dispute adjudication.

Next, we examine how good state governance outputs affect perceptions of gang legitimacy. Hypothesis 2 predicts how perceptions of good governance behavior by state actors will be associated with decreased nonstate actor legitimacy. Here, we use the same indicators of state governance – having a formal bank account, confidence in the police, and seeing a link between voting and service provision – but look at the relationship between those factors and the measures of gang legitimacy: relying on gangs to adjudicate disputes, and reporting gangs generally do more good than harm. These estimates are reported in Models 4–5. We find that respondents who report confidence in the police are significantly less likely to report using gangs to adjudicate a dispute. Somewhat counterintuitively, those who report seeing a link between voting and state service provision are more likely to report gangs are not harmful. One explanation for this pattern is those respondents are satisfied with the status quo, and as a result, are less likely to view gangs as a threat.

Having established that good state governance output is correlated with better assessments of state legitimacy (Models 1–3) and lower assessments of nonstate legitimacy (Models 4–5), we now turn to see how state legitimacy affects approval of lynching (Models 6–7). Our theory implies that those who see the state as legitimate are less likely to approve of lynching (Hypothesis 6). We use two measures of lynching: first, whether the respondent thinks lynching is generally preferred over state justice (Lynch Approve); second, a more specific scenario of whether they believe it is appropriate for neighbors to kill a thief (Thief Lynch

---

[135] We use these three indicators to capture different aspects of state "health": engagement with the formal banking sector indicates contract and property rights enforcement; confidence in the police measures the strength of police-society relations; and assessment of the link between voting and services is a measure of the state of democratic accountability. All models include commune fixed effects.

[136] Response choices are described earlier in the section; we code State Dispute Adjudication = 1 if the respondent selected agents of the government or state. We code Gang Dispute Adjudication = 1 if the respondent chose either baz, bandi, or brigade.

Approve). As predicted, respondents who report indicators of positive state legitimacy are significantly less likely to approve of lynching. For example, those who believe taxes are important are about 9.2 percentage points less likely to approve of lynching, and 15.1 percentage points less likely to approve of lynching a thief. Among those who support restoring the Haitian Army, we see a 20.1 percentage point decrease in the likelihood of approving of lynching, and a 16.8 percentage point decrease in the likelihood of approving the lynching a thief.

Overall, we take the estimates in Table 4.2 to illustrate that good performance by the state boosts state legitimacy, and may minimally diminish gang legitimacy. These positive state legitimacy indicators also translate into significantly decreased approval for lynching. This is a normatively positive finding, and one that may shed light on why lynching is not more common. These results may also offer some guidance for how lynching may be curbed, to which we return in the Conclusion (Section 5).

4.5.2 Poor State Governance, Legitimacy, and Lynching

We now examine how abuses by the state affect perceptions of state and gang legitimacy, respectively, and approval of lynching. Hypothesis 3 predicts that state abuses will be associated with decreased state legitimacy and increased gang legitimacy. We also use identical models as those just discussed to highlight the inverse relationship between state legitimacy and lynching: poor state legitimacy is associated with increased approval of lynching.

In the top panel of Table 4.3, we use state abuse as a proxy for respondents viewing the state to be repressive. In particular, we use two indicators of state abuse – reporting experiences of state violence during the Aristide eras of instability and reporting exposure to abusive violence by police – and examine their correlation with the same three indicators of state legitimacy. As predicted by Hypothesis 1, in Models 1–3, we observe that reporting experiences of state repression or police abuse is associated with a consistent, negative association with each of our indicators of state legitimacy. These negative perceptions are statistically significant for state repression, and in one of the specifications of police violence (Model 3).

Turning to how state abuses affect gang legitimacy, evidence is consistent with Hypothesis 3, which predicts state oppression can bolster positive perceptions of gangs. In Models 4–5, we estimate the effects of negative experiences with state agents of violence on willingness to go to gangs to solve disputes and viewing gangs as not harmful. In particular, we note that having had experience with violence during the Aristide crises periods increases the likelihood a respondent reports gangs are not harmful by nearly 35 percent. We see that

Table 4.3 State Abuses and Gang Governance on Legitimacy and Support for Lynching

	State Legitimacy			Gang Legitimacy		Lynching	
	(1)	(2)	(3)	(4)	(5)	(6)	(7)
	Taxes	State Dispute Adjudication	Restore Army	Gang Dispute Adjudication	Gangs Not Harmful	Lynch Approve	Thief Lynch Approve
Aristide Violence	−0.188***	−0.213***	−0.274***	−0.00395	0.349***	−0.0938***	−0.145***
	(0.0614)	(0.0774)	(0.0486)	(0.0297)	(0.0780)	(0.0348)	(0.0381)
Police Violence Exposure	−0.0706	−0.0262	−0.0932**	0.0332*	0.0653	0.0123	0.0338
	(0.0449)	(0.0701)	(0.0402)	(0.0190)	(0.0789)	(0.0216)	(0.0238)
Taxes important						−0.0938***	−0.145***
						(0.0348)	(0.0381)
State Dispute Resolution						0.0123	0.0338
						(0.0216)	(0.0238)
Army Restoration						−0.213***	−0.132**
						(0.0590)	(0.0530)
Constant	0.761***	0.810***	0.939***	0.0645**	0.249***	0.556***	0.712***
	(0.0519)	(0.0852)	(0.0344)	(0.0319)	(0.0693)	(0.0701)	(0.0730)
Observations	912	912	872	912	369	856	866
R-squared	0.077	0.032	0.117	0.029	0.276	0.064	0.085
Controls	Yes	Yes	Yes	Yes	Yes	Yes	Yes

	(1)	(2)	(3)	(4)	(5)	(6)	(7)
Gang Security Provision	-0.0782	-0.107	0.00530	0.117**	0.102		
	(0.0690)	(0.126)	(0.0334)	(0.0535)	(0.0671)		
Non-violent Gang services (count)	0.0356	0.0266	0.0135	0.0651**	0.0861***		
	(0.0447)	(0.0453)	(0.0165)	(0.0280)	(0.0248)		
Gang Dispute Adjudication						0.376**	0.223**
						(0.144)	(0.110)
Gangs not bad						0.129**	0.131**
						(0.0523)	(0.0647)
Constant	0.718***	0.776***	0.874***	0.0485*	0.277***	0.197***	0.422***
	(0.0577)	(0.0844)	(0.0422)	(0.0262)	(0.0767)	(0.0627)	(0.0819)
Observations	912	912	872	912	369	364	364
R-squared	0.061	0.026	0.013	0.164	0.259	0.119	0.178
Controls	Yes	Yes	Yes	Yes	Yes	Yes	Yes

Note: Standard errors clustered at the PSU in parentheses. All models include commune level fixed effects. ***p<0.01, **p<0.05, *p<0.1. Controls included are: gender, education level, age, and church attendance. Survey questions not already described in the text were as follows: Aristide Violence: Respondent reported they or a member of their family experienced injuries or death in relation to one of the periods of instability regarding Aristide: "Some people in this commune experienced injuries or deaths as a result of the unrest in 1991–1994 when the president was removed from power. Have you or your family (mom, dad, sisters, brothers, and sons and daughters)?" and "Some people in this commune experienced violence as a result of the unrest in 2004–2006 when the president was removed from office for the second time. Did your family?"; Police Violence Exposure: "Some people in this neighborhood may have experienced violence (injury or death) as a result of the police within the last five years. Have you or your family (mom, dad, sisters, brothers, and sons and daughters)?" Gang security provision =1 if the respondent lists *baz, bandi,* or *brigade* as one of the actors that provides them security. Non-violent gang services count is the count (0,3) of services (water, road repair, trash collection) the respondent reports are provided to them by gangs (*baz, bandi,* or *brigade*).

respondents who report having been exposed to police violence increases the likelihood of expressing a preference for gangs to solve disputes by 3.3 percent. Taken together, these results provide strong evidence in support of the hypothesized link between state abuses and the erosion of legitimacy for the state and increased legitimacy for gangs.

We next turn to investigating how attitudes about state legitimacy affect support for lynching. Hypothesis 6 predicts individuals who do not view the state as legitimate are more likely to approve of lynching. Models 6–7 report the identical estimates as in Table 4.2. We display them again here to illustrate the other side of this relationship, in the context of state abuses: among individuals with poor evaluations of state legitimacy, approval of lynching increases significantly. These findings suggest that the state has substantial control over how it fares in terms of mass perceptions of its legitimacy.

4.5.3 Good Gang Governance, Legitimacy, and Lynching

Table 4.2 and the top panel of Table 4.3 highlighted how the state has a large measure of influence over how it is perceived, but what about gangs? Here we focus on how gang governance activities affect gang and state legitimacy, and how gang legitimacy drives approval of lynching. We focus on two indicators of gang service provision: security services and non-violent social services. We code gang security provision as 1 when respondents name gangs as providing them security; non-violent gang services provision is a count variable (0,3) that sums the number of services the respondent reports are provided to them by gangs (water, sanitation, and road).

In the bottom panel of Table 4.3, we conduct an analysis with gangs similar to the one we did with the state's governance activities in Table 4.2 and the top panel of Table 4.3. First, we look at how gang service provision affects attitudes about gang legitimacy, as measured by going to gangs to resolve disputes and reporting that gangs are not harmful (Models 4–5). Hypothesis 1, as applied to gangs, predicts good governance activities should increase gang legitimacy. The results show that both forms of governance activities increase gang legitimacy. These are consistent with the sentiments expressed by one of our focus group participants who stated, "[Gangs] protect the area a lot. They protect my husband when he is driving home and block people who are not from the neighborhood. This is a good thing, from my perspective."[137]

In Models 1–3, we test whether gang service provision has any effect on indicators of state legitimacy (Hypothesis 4). We do not find evidence that

---

[137] Focus Group 3, Port-au-Prince, May 15, 2017.

gang activities influence perceptions of the state. This may be because the state is seen as the actor who *ought* to provide governance, which is consistent with our survey experiment in Section 4.6.

Finally, in Models 6–7, we estimate the link between gang legitimacy and general approval of lynching, and for thieves in particular. Consistent with Hypothesis 7, across all measures, we see an unambiguous link between receiving services from gangs and increased approval of lynching.

4.5.4 Lack of State or Gang Governance, Legitimacy, and Lynching

We have shown how state governance, gang governance, and state abuses affect state and gang legitimacy, and how state legitimacy and gang legitimacy are linked to support for lynching. We now look at a special case: what happens when neither the state nor gangs seem to be reliable governors, forcing community members to turn to self-help governance. In the analyses that follow, we look first at how increasing reliance on neighbors for service provision affects state legitimacy and gang legitimacy, and in turn approval of lynching. Hypothesis 8 predicts that in these pockets of self-governance, lynching support should increase.

In the top panel of Table 4.4, we measure self-help governance by the number of services that respondents report are provided by their neighbors. This varies from 0 to a maximum of 4 (security, water, trash, and roads). In Models 1–3, we show how increasing self-help governance affects the state. In general, we find no strong relationship – but as more services are provided by neighbors, respondents become significantly less likely to support restoring the Haitian Army. Next, in Models 4–5, we look at how self-governance affects gang legitimacy, finding no strong relationship, as we hypothesized.

Finally, we test how self-help governance is associated with approval of lynching. We theorized that those who rely on self-help governance are likely to feel comfortable with delegating justice to neighbors, leading to approval of lynching. Indeed, Models 6–7 highlight the strength of this relationship. In Model 6, each additional service a respondent reports being provided by their neighbors increases the likelihood of approving of lynching by about 5.1 percentage points. In Model 7, for each additional service provided by neighbors, respondents are 2.7 percentage points more likely to approve of lynching of thieves.

As an additional exploration of self-help governance, we focus on the respondents who report that *all* services are provided by their neighbors. In the bottom panel of Table 4.4, we look at how these forty-eight respondents

Table 4.4 Reliance on Neighbors for Services on Legitimacy and Support for Lynching

| | State Legitimacy | | | Gang Legitimacy | | | Lynching | |
	(1)	(2)	(3)	(4)	(5)	(6)	(7)
	Taxes	State Dispute Adjudication	Restore Army	Gang Dispute Adjudication	Gangs Not Harmful	Lynch Approve	Thief Lynch Approve
Neighbors Provide (count)	0.0169	−0.00926	−0.0185**	0.00214	0.00687	0.0505***	0.0272*
	(0.0147)	(0.0175)	(0.00886)	(0.00530)	(0.0255)	(0.0140)	(0.0145)
Constant	0.692***	0.780***	0.901***	0.0674	0.310***	0.253***	0.496***
	(0.0522)	(0.0892)	(0.0453)	(0.0405)	(0.0968)	(0.0550)	(0.0540)
Observations	912	912	872	912	369	895	904
R-squared	0.061	0.025	0.019	0.023	0.228	0.051	0.059
Controls	Yes	Yes	Yes	Yes	Yes	Yes	Yes

	(1)	(2)	(3)	(4)	(5)	(6)	(7)
	Taxes	State Dispute Adjudication	Restore Army	Gang Dispute Adjudication	Gangs Not Harmful	Lynch Approve	Thief Lynch Approve
Neighbors Provide All	0.0192	0.0145	−0.0795	0.0204	0.0776	0.262***	0.271***
	(0.0943)	(0.0814)	(0.0600)	(0.0301)	(0.0716)	(0.0715)	(0.0668)
Constant	0.713***	0.767***	0.879***	0.0693*	0.320***	0.308***	0.520***
	(0.0560)	(0.0861)	(0.0421)	(0.0361)	(0.0815)	(0.0495)	(0.0520)
Observations	912	912	872	912	369	895	904
R-squared	0.059	0.024	0.016	0.023	0.229	0.047	0.068
Controls	Yes	Yes	Yes	Yes	Yes	Yes	Yes

Note: Standard errors clustered at the PSU in parentheses. ***p<0.01, **p<0.05, *p<0.1, Controls included are: gender, education level, age, and church attendance. Neighbors Provide Count is the count (0,4) of services (security, water, road repair, trash collection) the respondent reports are provided to them by their neighbors. Neighbors Provide All = 1 if respondent reported all services (security, water, road repair, trash collection) were provided to them by their neighbors.

assess the state, gangs, and lynching. Because this is a relatively small set of respondents, any correlations will be difficult to detect. In Models 1–5, self-help governance seems to have little effect on the assessments of gang legitimacy and state legitimacy. However, in Models 6–7, self-help governance increases approval of lynching by about 27 percentage points. Substantively, this means those living in communities of Port-au-Prince where residents are forced to rely on neighbors for all services are overwhelmingly more likely to support lynching, both in general and for thieves.

4.6 Who Ought to be Providing Governance?

Our survey evidence points to relatively poor performance by the state for many respondents, as well as some indicators of the vulnerability of the state's status. Given the primacy of the state as the legitimate governance provider in the theoretical literature, we sought to explore whether the state is also dominant in the minds of local citizens as the entity that ought to be governing despite its present failures. To do so, we embedded a small survey experiment to determine whether priming respondents about national vs. local governance affects their responses concerning service provision by nonstate actors (especially reports of non-violent services by violent nonstate actors). Within each cluster, we administered each of the treatment primes described below.[138]

Our experiment consisted of two treatment primes and one control. Delivery was randomized within each cluster.

- Half of the sample received a control phrase prior to questions about service provision consisting of a brief introduction: "Now I'd like to talk to you about services."
- In 25 percent of the sample, enumerators delivered the following prime regarding *local governance*: "Some people believe that life is improved and security is increased when local people and many local groups are involved in governing the neighborhood, including making decisions, providing justice, solving problems, and offering resources, as opposed to the national government doing these things. Who do you think does the best job at governing the neighborhood: local groups, the national government, or a mix?"
- The remaining 25 percent of respondents received a similar prime, but one emphasizing the link between the *national government* and services: "Some people believe that life is improved and security is increased with just the national government governing the neighborhood, including making decisions, providing justice, solving problems and offering resources, rather than

---

[138] In calculating statistical power, we assumed geographic covariates account for 0.4 of variation, a treatment effect size of 0.27 sd, P= 0.8 power to detect a treatment effect, with $\alpha = 0.05$.

Table 4.5 Priming of State Governance on Reports of Nonstate Service
Provision

	(1)	(2)
	Report Gang Provision of Non-Violent Services	**Report Gang Provision of Non-Violent Services**
Local Prime	−0.0338	−0.0271
	(0.0406)	(0.0796)
National Prime	−0.130***	−0.329***
	(0.0409)	(0.0803)
Constant	0.199***	0.353***
	(0.0554)	(0.105)
Observations	912	500
R-squared	0.206	0.275
Controls	Yes	Yes
Sample	Full	Gangs Observed

Note: Standard errors in parentheses. ***p<0.01, **p<0.05, *p<0.1

locals and many local groups. Who do you think does the best job at governing the neighborhood: local groups, the national government, or a mix?"[139]

In Table 4.5 we display estimates to determine whether there might be
a difference in the likelihood of reporting non-violent service provision by
gangs based on the prime. We find that respondents who received the prime
about the role of the national government in providing governance were significantly less likely to report gang provision of non-violent services. This effect
is even larger when the sample is restricted to areas where gangs were reported
to be operating (Model 2).[140] While these findings are only suggestive, they
provide initial evidence that the state has a clear advantage in respondents'
minds about who *should* provide services, with only a light informational prime.

While the order of the items in the survey prevents us from analyzing the
prime's effect on attitudes about lynching, these results offer potentially hopeful
paths forward for changes in attitudes once the state improves service provision
to respondents in contested or ungoverned areas. In focus groups, respondents

---

[139] One concern might be that reporting is related to the presence of gangs. In Table A.2 in the
Online Appendix, we demonstrate there is no evidence that treatment status affects reporting the
presence of gangs.

[140] Gang presence is as observed by our enumerators. The correlation between respondent reports
and enumerator observations is 0.51. The results are substantively identical if we use respondent
reports of gang presence.

were deeply dissatisfied with the state's performance. One participant remarked, "Most of the government agencies are negligent and not effective."[141] However, we also find evidence that despite its current record, the Haitian state is still seen as a credible potential governance provider. As another participant remarked, "The government wastes a huge amount of money. But I'd still rather have the government take care of services."[142]

4.7 Summary of Main Results

In this section, we have analyzed the hypotheses derived from our core theory, examining at a local level the links between gang and state legitimacy and the emergence of lynching. Several key findings provide evidence for our theory. First, we find that when the state is viewed as providing effective governance, respondents rate its legitimacy as high and gang legitimacy as low. Those who assess the state as legitimate also strongly disapprove of lynching.

Next, we find that state abuses – in the form of political violence and police abuses – degrade the state's legitimacy, but do not consistently increase gang legitimacy. In turn, poor state legitimacy increases support for lynching as a practice.

Turning to the downstream effects of gang governance in the form of service provision, we find that service provision increases assessments of gang legitimacy, but does not consistently diminish state legitimacy. Those who assess gangs as legitimate, however, are also more likely to approve of lynching.

Where neighbors resort to self-help governance – relying on each other, rather than the state or gangs – neither the state nor gangs are seen as legitimate. Moreover, those who rely on self-help governance report high levels of approval of lynching.

Finally, we demonstrate that even under conditions in which governance is insufficient and the state is weak, the state remains the actor that respondents think *ought* to provide governance. While we cannot make a direct link to approval of lynching, an extension of our other results suggests that the more, and more reliably, state services are provided, the more support for lynching should decline.[143]

---

[141] Focus Group 3 participant, Port-au-Prince, May 16, 2017.   [142] Ibid.

[143] While we view the state and the gangs in a type of competition with each other, and argue that our evidence supports this argument, Kivland (2020: 18–19) presents a provocative opposing argument: she proposes "a dialectical rather than an oppositional framework, in which state power is not presumed to exist and be challenged by a nonstate force but is rather in the process of being continually eluded, embraced, and constituted by it. ... Insofar as the baz sees itself as governing in conjunction with the government and NGOs, it makes little sense to position it in a tug-of-war with these entities."

5 Conclusion: Implications for Theory and Policy

"A hungry dog doesn't play." [Chenn grangou pa jwe.]
– Haitian proverb, quoted by focus group participant, Port-au-Prince[144]

Lynching as we have defined it is a form of spontaneous collective violence, perpetrated by unorganized groups, with the aim of controlling crime and establishing local order. When someone who transgresses against a community can be put to death quickly by fellow citizens – brutally and with broad support and approval – this raises a number of concerns at the intersection of legitimacy and governance.

Research on lynching at the comparative global scale is still nascent, and many open questions remain. For instance, what are the long-term political and social consequences of widespread lynching for individuals and societies? Once it begins, how is the practice eventually mitigated or curbed? How do particular forms of violence – such as necklacing the victim – spread across countries and cultures, and why? While some of these questions are well beyond the scope of this Element, here we reflect on what our results suggest about (1) the long-term consequences of lynching and (2) how lynching might be stopped once it has become common. Finally, we consider how our findings speak to broad questions in political economy about state formation and decay, as well as the sources of accountability and justice. We also suggest a number of promising future paths for research.

5.1 Social and Political Consequences of Lynching

This analysis of lynching complements previous scholarship on the social aspects of extreme forms of collective political violence – including public gang rape (Cohen 2016), genocide (Straus 2007; Valentino 2005), witch trials (Leeson and Russ 2017), and "violent display," the "collective effort to stage violence for people to see, notice, or take in" (Fujii 2017). As we have argued throughout this Element, the adoption of modes of execution that require broad local participation are critical to sustaining the practice and imbuing it with community-level legitimacy and approval, or at least the perception of wide-spread approval.

A likely consequence of broad participation is that lynching, a type of collective targeting (Steele 2011), can entrench group identities, making the violence very challenging to halt once it has begun. Research on plausibly related forms of public group violence, such as gang rape, has found that these forms of atrocities create strong ties between perpetrators (Cohen 2016). As

---

[144] Focus Group 1, Port-au-Prince, May 15, 2017.

Littman and Paluck (2015: 81) write, participating in violence leads "to a cycle of violence in which group identification increases willingness to engage in violent behavior and perpetrating violence increases group identification." Finally, the role of psychological release is also a driver. It may be especially critical for communities with few other outlets for expression of frustration. This was apparent in Haiti, where some participate because they "want to beat the hell out of someone."[145] Interventions to mitigate lynching will need to take seriously this cycle of violence, and how strongly participants may have become attached to their self-perceptions as protectors of their communities.

Additionally, the common use of grisly methods – that require many participants and create "neighborhood" legitimacy for the practice – also might offer insights into how this type of behavior might be curbed. Because perpetrators are rarely identifiable, prosecution is difficult.[146] One path to break anonymity of lynching perpetrators is to use modern technology. For example, in Brazil, one participant in a lynching was identified in a cellphone video.[147] Social media and other efforts to identify those who participate may help reduce the anonymity that sustains the practice, offering a toehold for modern anti-lynching campaigns to hold perpetrators responsible and to reduce impunity. However, critically, our work shows that efforts to disrupt this collective action must also be coupled with good governance, including a robust judicial system.

In addition to the immediate consequences, there is good reason to suspect that areas where lynching is common will face long-term negative social and political consequences, even generations after lynching ceases. Scholars have found links between historically higher rates of lynching in the United States and a host of modern-day outcomes, including incarceration rates, housing discrimination, negative health consequences, and even higher rates of homicide (e.g., Probst et al. 2019; Weintraub 2016). While the causal linkages remain uncertain, the evidence suggests that lynching leaves a lasting negative impact on the immediate communities where it occurs.

---

[145] Authors' interview with local scholar, August 7, 2018

[146] Anonymity is not limited to cases of contemporary lynching; Ku Klux Klan hoods serve a similar purpose, particularly in legal settings where perpetrators feared prosecution. Allison Kinney, "How the Klan Got Its Hood," *The New Republic*, January 8, 2016: https://newrepublic .com/article/127242/klan-got-hood.

[147] Samantha Pearson and Luciana Magalhaes, "In Latin America, Awash in Crime, Citizens Impose Their Own Brutal Justice," *Wall Street Journal,* December 6, 2018: www.wsj.com /articles/in-a-continent-awash-in-crime-citizens-impose-their-own-brutal-justice-1544110959

5.2 How Does Lynching End?

Curbing lynching is not simply a matter of explicit prohibition; even the harshest laws that prohibit lynching are likely to be difficult to enforce. In some contexts, mistrust in the legal system is rampant, and is itself a major driver of lynching. This, combined with the fact that many of the states in which lynching is reported are still consolidating their democratic institutions, means it is unclear if a legal solution is likely to be effective. According to one study, Haitians understand "the law as an imposition of the powerful over the weak and not as a reflection of law and order" (INURED 2017: 26).

An instructive case may be the United States. The end of lynching in the United States was not the result of legal intervention. An anti-lynching law has never been passed in the United States, and it was not until December 2018 that the United States Senate finally passed an anti-lynching bill (as of this writing, it has not yet been passed by the House of Representatives or signed by the president.) There have been more than 200 failed anti-lynching bills since 1918; the Senate passed a resolution in 2005 apologizing for the lack of legal prohibitions on lynching. Scholars identify several competing explanations for the decline of lynching in the United States, including that lynching was replaced by a more efficient criminal justice system, as well as the expansion of the death penalty to meet public demand for capital punishment. As well, social pressure, particularly from journalists and activists such as Ida B. Wells, shifted norms about the acceptability of lynching. In addition, the Great Northward Migration of blacks depleted local supplies of inexpensive labor in the rural South, and economic concerns are thought to have spurred a reduction of violence (Bailey et al., 2011; Berg and Wendt 2011).

More generally, Berg and Wendt (2011) argue that three distinct conditions are necessary to halt lynching: the ability and willingness of the state to enforce its claim on the monopoly of violence; popular acceptance of this claim; and the belief that the criminal justice system is capable of enforcing the law and punishing criminals in accordance to popular expectations. In essence, a state must seek to "win hearts and minds" to convince local people that the police and judicial system are effective, sufficiently punitive, and fair enough to override an entrenched practice. This is a tall order when the state is so deeply mistrusted and neighbors routinely rely on self-help to solve problems, but our findings suggest that it is possible.

Authorities have made early attempts at turning the tide in Haiti. The UN rolled out an awareness campaign that included "sensitization sessions" with nearly 2,500 people involved in local governance, such as police and mayors. The campaign also highlighted anti-lynching messages in radio announcements, posters and leaflets. The UN's report on lynching (MINUSTAH 2017) recommends a number of policies that should be tried, including aggressive prosecution of all perpetrators, and witnesses who fail to help the victim; an education campaign for representatives of the legal system – from police to prosecutors – about their legal obligations to punish perpetrators of lynching; and calls for more systematic data collection. The report specifically laments the lack of data, which could be used to ask more nuanced questions and to test common arguments, such as public frustration with impunity as a driver of lynching.

5.3 Theoretical Implications

We now turn to implications that follow from our theory of how governance behavior and legitimacy create an environment in which lynching emerges and persists. If, as we demonstrate in Section 4, governance is an essential link in the chain that produces lynching, there are some conclusions that follow regarding trust in state agents.

5.3.1 State Capacity vs. State Legitimacy

Many accounts of lynching note the absence of a police presence as a partial explanation. For example, the common refrain that participants are "taking the law into their own hands" can imply that the police are not present to do so themselves. Some reports of community justice point directly to an inability of the government to control crime. Take Guatemala, where "many observers attributed the lynchings to continued public frustration with the failure of law enforcement and judicial authorities to guarantee security" (State Department Human Rights Report, Guatemala 2007). A 1985 State Department report on Brazil notes, "Numerous lynchings have been reported in the press and the phenomenon is apparently increasing. The greatest incidence of lynching takes place in the slums on the outskirts of major cities, a result of perceptions that police and court protection is unavailable." A purely state (and policing) capacity argument would predict the emergence of lynching in areas that are remote and difficult to access and monitor.

However, our theory also suggests lynching emerges not only from a lack of state *capacity*, but critically from a lack of state *legitimacy*. Lynching is reported in both urban and rural contexts, and available evidence from around the world points to a complicated interplay between the police, state capacity, and lynching. Lynching is sometimes reported in cases where the police are present and appear to be capable – but their authority is seen to be illegitimate. This dynamic is perhaps most stark when there is strong resistance to police efforts to curb lynching itself; for example, residents in Guatemala "attempted to lynch two women suspected of kidnapping . . . and burned patrol vehicles of police officers who intervened to prevent the lynchings" (State Department Human Rights Report, Guatemala 2007). Lynching can also occur when police actions to ensure accountability and punishment are not publicly accepted. For example, in Ecuador in 2002, after a man was arrested for murder, residents blocked the highway when the police attempted to move him to a different town, in apparent fear that the man would escape accountability. An estimated 3,500 residents surrounded the police station, threw the accused murderer off the second floor and then shot him (State Department Human Rights Report, Ecuador 2002).

A clear finding that emerges from our analysis is that where states provide good governance, they are perceived as legitimate and lynching is not viewed as an appropriate punishment mechanism. Should this practice emerge *only* in contexts in which the state and the instruments of state force (i.e., police, military) are absent or lack capacity, a clear policy remedy would be increased policing and a more robust police force. But if lynching occurs in areas where the state may be present but mistrusted, as we find, then merely increasing police presence will not mitigate the occurrence of lynching independent of concurrent policies that bolster state trust and legitimacy.

That community justice seems to be linked more closely to a lack of state *legitimacy* rather than merely a lack of state *capacity* is critical for understanding the process of state building and democratic consolidation. Our findings imply that fostering citizens' trust in the judicial system and police is as important as establishing the footprint and institutions of the state. As with counter-insurgency and the efforts to win "hearts and minds," our results show that the need to deliver services and build trust and confidence in the state are central to combatting lynching.[148]

This analysis also clarifies some challenges to curbing the practice of community justice once those institutions are well functioning. We observe high levels of lynching in states where, at least in some spheres, the courts operate well. However, in the sub-regions where lynching thrives, those courts are seen as untrustworthy, too slow, or corrupt. In these situations, the populations must be actively convinced that the state's institutions are reliable and accountable. Optimistically, the priming experiment at the end of Section 4 suggests that more information can shift perceptions of governance, potentially offering a pathway for anti-lynching campaigns.

---

[148] See US Army Field Manual 3-24 for an articulation of modern "Hearts and Minds" doctrine.

5.3.2 Identifying Where Lynching Is Likely to Thrive

Our theory also speaks to *where,* within countries, lynching is likely to emerge. Specifically, lynching seems most likely in neighborhoods where citizens are underserved by the state and are receiving basic services from nonstate actors (or at the very least, perceive that the services they receive are from nonstate sources). Where citizens are completely neglected by the state and its competitors, lynching may be most likely. While we do not consider whether this emerges in the context in which a *political* nonstate actor, such as a rebel group, competes directly with the state for political authority, we hypothesize that this would lead to a zero-sum competition over rightful rule potentially in the form of a rebel court system to rival the state's.

Our findings point to a common social solution: states must create and reliably provide community accountability and justice in settings where the rightful rule of the state is fundamentally degraded. Shifting away from lynching may be possible through both increasing provision of services and the consistent application of an unbiased justice system.

5.3.3 Changing Conventions and Disrupting Collective Action

The collective nature of the punishment is one of the critical features of lynching, and why we argue the practice is imbued with a sense of local legitimacy. In some instances of shifts in convention, change evolves over several generations.[149] While some tools – such as mass education campaigns – have proved successful combatting harmful practices, the severity and immediacy of lynching sets it apart from other potentially negative social conventions, such as female genital mutilation and foot binding. As a result, these prior efforts to shift harmful conventions offer useful lessons, but they may not be analogous to unraveling the problem of lynching.

We see evidence in Haiti that those who perceive themselves to be relatively vulnerable to the crimes lynching punishes – and who do not see themselves as potential victims of lynching – are potentially more likely to support it. This logic may explain why some evidence shows women disproportionately support lynching (Cooper and Wilke 2018). An intervention that follows is to focus

---

[149] Alternatively, change may happen quickly using targeted interventions; for example, the use of public contracts that dissuaded families from continuing practices such as foot binding and female genital mutilation (FGM) (Mackie 1996). In those cases, families agreed not to bind their daughters' feet or to cut their daughters and to prohibit their sons from marrying any woman with bound feet or FGM. The success of these campaigns is attributed to the ability to observe other families adhering to the agreement. However, features of lynching make a similar solution untenable, such as the swiftness of the event and the lack of ability for others to clearly identify instances of restraint or refusal to participate.

programs on reducing vulnerability, both real and perceived, by increasing measures to keep these sub-populations safe and to prosecute crimes committed against them. While the primary division in Haiti is along economic class, in different settings, vulnerable subgroups may be defined by religious, ethnic, or political cleavages. If part of the broad support that makes lynching self-sustaining and difficult to eliminate is a sense of vulnerability, then reducing this perception is central to undercutting the broad social support the practice enjoys.

5.4 Future Research

The specific method of justice and accountability we examine – lynching – opens up a set of questions about the emergence and persistence of local authority. This Element introduces and highlights the breadth and scope of the practice, but many theoretical and empirical questions remain unanswered, both about individual participation in the practice as well as its interaction with state entities. We hope future work will tackle these issues, and we highlight a number of promising avenues here.

First, the global dataset we present can provide a rich foundation for future research into the sources of cross-national variation. Studies could analyze the sources of variation across countries to evaluate the competing causes of lynchings and vigilante justice. Some potential variables – beyond development and poverty – that could be explored in future research include: food shortages, chronic theft, epidemic disease, police corruption, unemployment, previous civil war, colonial history, socioeconomic inequality, belief in witchcraft, weakness of statuary justice, honor culture, and public protests.[150]

Beyond explaining variation in the occurrence of lynching, studies could explore the transmission of *forms* of lynching violence across time and space. For instance, Jacobs and Schuetze (2011) argue that necklacing spread to Mozambique from Apartheid-era South Africa in part because participants understood this to be a form of violence used in political protest.[151] Others argue that necklacing also spread from South Africa to Haiti as a method of political protest (D'Adesky 1991). More generally, why particular types of atrocities become adopted is understudied.

Finally, while our cross-national data are useful, they are limited to one commonly used English-language source. Future research can supplement these data by coding reports from other sources including local newspapers and NGO reports.

---

[150] See Jacobs and Schuetze (2011) and Berg and Wendt (2011) for discussions of some of these ideas.

[151] See also Smith (2017) on necklacing by vigilante groups in South Africa over time.

Our study also suggests avenues for scholarship on the subnational level. Much still remains to be explored in terms of the micro dynamics of lynching. For example, who participates and why? What is the process of coming to judge a perpetrator as guilty? When might the accused be let free? In addition, there are open questions about the *aftermath* of lynching. For example, given the specter of punishing an innocent person, does an unwarranted lynching of a wrongly accused suspect make communities less likely to participate in lynchings in the future?

Survey research on lynching is sparse. Future research might employ indirect methods for eliciting truthful responses, such as the use of list experiments, to estimate direct participation. Survey experiments could also vary the alleged evidence against the accused to illuminate more about the micro dynamics regarding how attitudes about lynching are shaped. A survey experiment could assess whether someone seeing a crime versus hearing about a crime second-hand affects attitudes about whether lynching is appropriate. For example, García-Ponce et al. (2019) use survey experiments in Western Mexico to show the who is victimized has a stronger influence on support for vigilantism than the severity of the violence.

Finally, survey data are necessary to evaluate hypotheses that require information on people's perceptions of their security. One critical question for future research (that we do not fully explore here, due to data limitations) is that lynching emerges where state *legitimacy* is lacking, not necessarily where state *presence* is lacking; survey data could be used to show whether these factors are correlated.

5.5 Conclusion

This Element speaks to larger questions in the area of political economy, particularly around understanding state formation, consolidation, and decay. Scholars of international relations tend to focus on revisions to the state or its authority at moments of major transition (e.g., inter- or intrastate war, colonization, or independence). However, such major transitions are relatively rare. This Element highlights that a focus on local de facto governance can shed significant light on the realities and practices that arise outside of such major shifts in global authority. We show that within a single city, outside of an ongoing conflict, multiple entities may be working to provide services and build legitimacy. The lack of a state monopoly can cause significant anxiety among the population, leading to a host of negative social outcomes, including lynching.

Lynching is more frequent, and the patterns around its practice more persistent, than commonly recognized. Citizens in many parts of the modern world live in neighborhoods of – sometimes otherwise very stable – countries where lynching regularly occurs. Our cross-national data reveal a secular increase in reporting of lynching over time, as well as similarities in the mode and form of the practice across time and space. Our work in Haiti suggests that while this type of justice is not the public's first choice, it is generally interpreted as a necessary evil born of conditions where resources are scarce, and trust in formal governance mechanisms has been shaken or is eroded.

Taken together, these findings shed light on a disturbing and understudied form of political violence to understand how it emerges and how it is sustained. For policymakers, an increasing focus on community justice is particularly timely. Recent news has highlighted an increase in mob killings in several countries. If our results are correct – and lynching is closely linked to the degradation of legitimacy – there are inventions that states should consider, both to increase legitimacy and to prevent lynching.

Bibliography

Anderson, Terry Lee, and Peter Jensen Hill. 2004. *The Not So Wild, Wild West: Property Rights on the Frontier*. Stanford, CA: Stanford University Press.

Allen, Frederick. 2004. *A Decent, Orderly Lynching: The Montana Vigilantes*. Norman: University of Oklahoma Press.

Arias, Desmond Enrique. 2017. *Criminal Enterprises and Governance in Latin America and the Caribbean*. New York: Cambridge University Press.

Arjona, Ana. 2015. "Civilian Resistance to Rebel Governance," in *Rebel Governance in Civil War*, Ana Arjona, Nelson Kasfir, and Zachariah Mampilly, eds. New York: Cambridge University Press, pp. 180–202.

Bahney, Ben, Radha Iyengar, Patrick Johnston et al. 2013. "Insurgent Compensation: Evidence from Iraq." *American Economic Review* 103(3): 518–522.

Bailey, Amy Kate, Stewart E. Tolnay, E. M. Beck, and Jennifer D. Laird. 2011. "Targeting Lynch Victims: Social Marginality or Status Transgressions?" *American Sociological Review* 76(3): 412–436.

Barnes, Nicholas. 2017. "Criminal Politics: An Integrated Approach to the Study of Organized Crime, Politics and Violence," *Perspectives on Politics* 15(4): 967–987.

Bateson, Regina. 2017. "The Socialization of Civilians and Militia Members: Evidence from Guatemala." *Journal of Peace Research* 54(5): 634–647.

Bateson, Regina. 2019. "The Politics of Vigilantism." Unpublished manuscript, April 9.

Becker, David. 2010. "Gangs, Netwar, and Community Counterinsurgency in Haiti." *Prism* 2(3): 137–154. https://apps.dtic.mil/dtic/tr/fulltext/u2/1042710.pdf.

Berg, Louis-Alexandre. 2010. *Crime, Politics and Violence in Post-Earthquake Haiti*, Washington, DC: United States Institute of Peace. www.usip.org/publications/2010/10/crime-politics-and-violence-post-earthquake-haiti.

Berg, Manfred, and Simon Wendt. 2011. "Introduction: Lynching from an International Perspective," in *Globalizing Lynching History: Vigilantism and Extralegal Punishment from an International Perspective*, eds., Manfred Berg and Simon Wendt. New York: Palgrave Macmillan, pp. 1–18.

Berman, Eli. 2011. *Radical, Religious, and Violent: The New Economics of Terrorism*. Princeton: Princeton University Press.

Cammett, Melani. 2014. *Compassionate Communalism: Welfare and Sectarianism in Lebanon.* Ithaca: Cornell University Press.

Cammett, Melani, and Lauren Morris MacLean. 2014. *The Politics of Non-state Social Welfare.* Ithaca: Cornell University Press.

Carrigan, William, and Christopher Waldrep. 2013. *Swift to Wrath: Lynching in Global Historical Perspective.* Charlottesville: University of Virginia Press.

Chesler, Phyllis. 2010. "Worldwide Trends in Honor Killings." *Middle East Quarterly* 17(2): 3–11.

Cohen, Dara Kay. 2013. "Explaining Rape during Civil War: Cross-National Evidence (1980–2009)." *American Political Science Review* 107(3): 461–477.

Cohen, Dara Kay. 2016. *Rape during Civil War.* Ithaca: Cornell University Press.

Cohen, Dara Kay, Amelia Hoover Green, and Elisabeth Wood. 2012. "Is Wartime Rape Declining on a Global Scale? We Don't Know and It Doesn't Matter," *Political Violence @ a Glance,* November 1. http://politicalviolenceataglance .org/ 192012/11/01/is-wartime-rape-declining-on-a-global-scale-we-dont-know -and-it-doesnt-matter/.

Cohen, Dara Kay, and Ragnhild Nordås. 2014. "Sexual Violence in Armed Conflict: Introducing the SVAC dataset, 1989–2009." *Journal of Peace Research* 51(3): 418–428.

Cohen, Dara Kay, and Danielle F. Jung. 2018. "Fatalities and Lethal Violence in Port-au-Prince (2002–2017)." dx.doi.org/10.7910/DVN/KX5JRF Harvard Dataverse, V3.

Commission on Global Governance. 1995. *Our Global Neighborhood.* New York: Oxford University Press.

Cooper, Jasper, and Anna Wilke. 2018. "'Thief!' Explaining Support for Mob Vigilantism in Africa and Melanesia." Unpublished manuscript, presented at APSA, Boston.

Coppedge, Michael, John Gerring, Carl Henrik Knutsen et al. 2018. "V-Dem Codebook v8." *Varieties of Democracy (V-Dem) Project.* www.v-dem.net /media/filer_public/e0/7f/e07f672b-b91e-4e98-b9a3-78f8cd4de696/v-dem_ codebook_v8.pdf.

Cunningham, Kathleen, Katherine Sawyer, and Reyko Huang. 2018. "Voting for Militants: Rebel Elections in Civil War." Unpublished manuscript. http://www .kathleengallaghercunningham.com/uploads/4/5/5/8/45589607/voting_for_mi litants_web.pdf.

D'Adesky, Anne-Christine. 1991. "Haiti: Pére Lebrun in Context." *Report on the Americas* 25(3): 7–9.

Davenport, Christian, and Patrick Ball. 2002. "Views to a Kill: Exploring the Implications of Source Selection in the Case of Guatemalan State Terror, 1977–1995." *Journal of Conflict Resolution* 46(3): 427–450.

Dubois, Laurent. 2005. *Avengers of the New World: The Story of the Haitian Revolution*. Cambridge: Harvard University Press.

Édouard, Roberson, and Arnaud Dandoy. 2016. *Vigilantism in Haiti: Manifestations of Non- governmental Forms of Protection in Urban Environments Undergoing Humanitarian Crisis*. Port-au- Prince, OXFAM-IIED.

Ellickson, Robert. 1994. *Order Without Law: How Neighbors Settle Disputes*. Cambridge: Harvard University Press.

Fatton, Jr., Robert. 2007. *The Roots of Haitian Despotism*. Boulder: Lynne Reiner.

Fariss, Christopher, Fridolin Linder, Zachary Jones et al. 2015. "Human Rights Texts: Converting Human Rights Primary Source Documents into Data," Harvard Dataverse. https://doi.org/10.7910/DVN/IAH8OY.

Fearon, James, and David Laitin. 2003. "Ethnicity, Insurgency, and Civil War. *American Political Science Review*, 97(1): 75–90.

Franklin, Karen. 2004. "Enacting Masculinity: Antigay Violence and Group Rape as Participatory Theater." *Sexuality Research & Social Policy* 1(2): 25–40.

Fujii, Lee Ann. 2017. "'Talk of the Town': Explaining Pathways to Participation in Violent Display." *Journal of Peace Research* 54(5): 661–673.

García-Ponce, Omar, Lauren Young, and Thomas Zeitzoff. 2019. "Anger and Support for Vigilante Justice in Mexico's Drug War." Unpublished Manuscript. http://www.laurenelyssayoung.com/wp-content/uploads/2018/08/Mexico_ViolenceAnger_Article_v4.pdf.

Gibbons, Jonathan. 2013. "Global Study on Homicide," United National Office of Drugs and Crime (Vienna). www.unodc.org/documents/gsh/pdfs/2014_GLOBAL_HOMICIDE_BOOK_web.pdf.

Gibney, Mark, Linda Cornett, Reed Wood, Peter Haschke, Daniel Arnon, and Attilio Pisanò. 2018. The Political Terror Scale 1976–2017. http://www.politicalterrorscale.org.

Godoy, Angelina Snodgrass. 2006. *Popular Injustice: Violence, Community, and Law in Latin America*. Stanford: Stanford University Press.

Goldstein, Daniel. 2003. "'In Our Own Hands': Lynching, Justice, and the Law in Bolivia." *American Ethnologist* 30(1): 22–43.

Goldstein, Judith, Miles Kahler, Robert O. Keohane, and Anne-Marie Slaughter. 2000. "Introduction: Legalization and World Politics." *International Organization* 54(3): pp. 385–399.

Gordon, Grant, and Lauren Young. 2017. "Cooperation, Information, and Keeping the Peace: Civilian Engagement with Peacekeepers in Haiti." *Journal of Peace Research* 54(1): 64–79.

Green, Donald, Jack Glaser, and Andrew Rich. 1998. "From Lynching to Gay Bashing: The Elusive Connection between Economic Conditions and Hate Crime." *Journal of Personality and Social Psychology* 75(1): 82–92.

Gunderson, Anna. 2018. "Why Do States Privatize Their Prisons? The Unintended Consequences of Inmate Litigation." Unpublished manuscript: http://www.annagunderson.com/uploads/1/5/3/2/15320172/jmpsept4.pdf

Heger, Lindsay, and Danielle Jung. 2017. "Negotiating with Rebels: The Effect of Rebel Service Provision on Conflict Negotiations" *Journal of Conflict Resolution* 61(6): 1203–1229

Hobbes, Thomas. 1651. *Leviathan*. MacPherson (1968).

Hovland, Carl Iver, and Robert Sears. 1940. "Minor Studies of Aggression: VI. Correlation of Lynching with Economic Indices." *The Journal of Psychology* 9(2): 301–310.

INURED (Interuniversity Institute for Research and Development). 2017. "Republic of Haiti: Country of Origin Information Paper," commissioned by the UNHCR, August. www.inured.org/uploads/2/5/2/6/25266591/unchr_coi_haiti_final_redacted_report_inured.pdf.

Jacobs, Carolien, and Christy Schuetze. 2011. "'Justice with Our Own Hands': Lynching, Poverty, Witchcraft, and the State in Mozambique." In *Globalizing Lynching History: Vigilantism and Extralegal Punishment from an International Perspective*, eds., Manfred Berg and Simon Wendt. New York: Palgrave Macmillan, (pp. 225–241).

Jo, Hyeran. 2018. "Compliance with International Humanitarian Law by Non-State Armed Groups: How Can It Be Improved?" *Yearbook of International Humanitarian Law* 19: 63–88.

Johnston, Patrick, Jacob Shapiro, Howard Shatz et al. 2016. *Foundations of the Islamic State: Management, Money and Terror in Iraq, 2005–2010*. RAND Corporation.

Keene, Edward. 2002. *Beyond the Anarchical Society: Grotius, Colonialism and Order in World Politics*. New York: Cambridge University Press.

Kenney, Michael. 2007. *From Pablo to Osama: Trafficking and Terrorist Networks, Government Bureaucracies, and Competitive Adaptation*. University Park: Pennsylvania State University Press.

Kahler, Miles, and David Lake 2003. "Globalization and Governance." In *Governance in a Global Economy: Political Authority in Transition*, Kahler, Miles and David A. Lake, eds. Princeton: Princeton University Press. Chapter 1, pp. 1–32.

Keohane, Robert. 2002. *Power and Governance in a Partially Globalized World*. London: Routledge.

Kivland, Chelsey. 2020. *Street Sovereigns: Young Men and the Makeshift State in Urban Haiti*. Ithaca: Cornell University Press. (manuscript forthcoming)

Kolbe, Athena. 2013. "Revisiting Haiti's Gangs and Organized Violence," Working Paper 147 Households in Conflict Network. www.hicn.org/word press/wp-content/uploads/2012/06/HiCN-WP-147.pdf.

Krasner, Stephen. 1993. "Westphalia and All That." In *Ideas and Foreign Policy: Beliefs, Institutions, and Political Change*, eds., Judith Goldstein and Robert Keohane. Ithaca: Cornell University Press. Chapter 9, pp. 235–264.

Krasner, Stephen. 1999. *Sovereignty: Organized Hypocrisy*. Princeton: Princeton University Press.

Krasner, Stephen D. 2004. "Sharing Sovereignty: New Institutions for Collapsed and Failing States" *International Security* 29(4): 85–120

Krasner, Stephen, and Thomas Risse. 2014. "External Actors, State-Building, and Service Provision in Areas of Limited Statehood." *Governance* 27(4): 545–567.

Lake, David. 1996. "Anarchy, Hierarchy, and the Variety of International Relations," *International Organization* 50(1): 1–33.

Lake, David A. 1999. *Entangling Relations: American Foreign Policy in its Century*, Princeton: Princeton University Press.

Lake, David. 2009. *Hierarchy in International Relations*. Ithaca: Cornell University Press.

Lake, David. 2010. "Rightful Rulers: Authority, Order, and the Foundations of Global Governance." *International Studies Quarterly* 54(3): 587–613.

Lansing, J. Stephen. 2006. *Perfect Order: Recognizing Complexity in Bali*. Princeton: Princeton University Press.

LeBas, Adrienne. 2013. "Violence and Urban Order in Nairobi, Kenya and Lagos, Nigeria." *Studies in Comparative International Development* 48(3): 240–262.

Leeson, Peter. 2007. "An-*arrgh*-chy: The Law and Economics of Pirate Organization," *Journal of Political Economy* 115(6): 1049–1094.

Leeson, Peter, and Jacob W. Russ. 2017. "Witch Trials." *The Economic Journal* 128(613): 2066–2105.

Lessing, Benjamin. 2015. "Logics of Violence in Criminal War." *Journal of Conflict Resolution* 59(8): 1486–1516.

Lessing, Benjamin. 2017. "Counterproductive Punishment: How Prison Gangs Undermine State Authority." *Rationality and Society* 29(3): 257–297.

Lessing, Benjamin, and Graham Denyer Willis. 2019. "Legitimacy in Criminal Governance: Managing a Drug Empire from Behind Bars." *American Political Science Review* (forthcoming).

Levitt, Steven, and Sudhir Venkatesh. 2000. "An Economic Analysis of a Drug-selling Gang's Finances." *Quarterly Journal of Economics* 115(3): 755–789.

Littman, Rebecca, and Elizabeth Levy Paluck. 2015. "The Cycle of Violence: Understanding Individual Participation in Collective Violence." *Political Psychology* 36(S1): 79–99.

Loyle, Cyanne, and Helga Malmin Binningsbø. 2018. "Justice During Armed Conflict: A New Dataset on Government and Rebel Strategies." *Journal of Conflict Resolution* 62(2): 442–466.

Mackie, Gerry. 1996. "Ending Footbinding and Infibulation: A Convention Account" *American Sociological Review* 61(6): 999–1017

Mampilly, Zachariah Cherian. 2011. *Rebel Rulers: Insurgent Governance and Civilian Life During War*. Ithaca: Cornell University Press.

MINUSTAH/Haut-Commissariat des Nations Unies aux droits de l'homme. 2017. "Bay tèt yo jistis: Se faire justice soi-même ou le règne de l'impunité en Haïti," Janvier. www.ohchr.org/Documents/Countries/HT/170117Rapport_Se_faire_ju stice_soimeme_FR.pdf.

MINUJUSTH. 2019. "La Saline: Justice pour les victimes l'Etat a l'obligation de proteger tous les citoyens." https://minujusth.unmissions.org/sites/default/files/minujusth_hcdh_rapport_la_saline.pdf.

Moncada, Eduardo. 2019. "The Politics of Criminal Victimization: Pursuing and Resisting Power," *Perspectives on Politics*. doi: 10.1017/S153759271900029X.

Moore, E. F. 1964. "The Firing Squad Synchronization Problem." In *Sequential Machines, Selected Papers*, E. F. Moore, ed. Reading, MA: Addison-Wesley, pp. 213–214.

More, Sir Thomas. 1845. *Utopia: Or the Happy Republic: A Philosophical Romance*. London: Joseph Rickerby.

Mueller, John. 2000. "The Banality of 'Ethnic War.'" *International Security* 25 (1): 42–70.

Ormhaug, Christin Marsh, Patrick Meier, and Helga Hernes. 2009. "Armed Conflict Deaths Disaggregated by Gender," PRIO Paper. Oslo: PRIO. www.prio.org/utility/DownloadFile.ashx?id=411&type=publicationfile.

Osorio, Javier, Livia Schubiger, and Michael Weintraub. 2019. "Historical Legacies of Conflict: From the Cristero Rebellion to Self-Defense Forces in Mexico," working paper.

Pfeifer, Michael, ed. 2017. *Global Lynching and Collective Violence: Volume 1: Asia, Africa, and the Middle East*. University of Illinois Press.

Phillips, Brian. 2015. "How Does Leadership Decapitation Affect Violence?" *Journal of Politics* 77(2): 324–336.

Probst, Janice, Saundra Glover, and Victor Kirksey. 2019. "Strange Harvest: A Cross-Sectional Ecological Analysis of the Association Between Historic Lynching Events and 2010–2014 County Mortality Rates." *Journal of Racial and Ethnic Health Disparities* 6(1): 143–152.

Reno, William. 2011. *Warfare in Independent Africa*. New York: Cambridge University Press.

Risse, Thomas, and Eric Stollenwerk. 2018a. "Legitimacy in Areas of Limited Statehood." *Annual Review of Political Science* 21.

Risse, Thomas, and Eric Stollenwerk. 2018b. "Limited Statehood Does Not Equal Civil War." *Daedalus* 147(1): 104–115.

Scharpf, Fritz. 2007. "Reflections on Multilevel Legitimacy," MPIfG Working Paper 07/3, Max-Planck-Institut für Gesellschaftsforschung, Köln Max Planck Institute for the Study of Societies, Cologne, July.

Schwartz, Timothy. 2008. *Travesty in Haiti: A True Account of Christian Missions, Orphanages, Fraud, Food Aid and Drug Trafficking*. North Charleston, SC: Booksurge Publishing.

Shapiro, Jacob. 2013. *The Terrorist's Dilemma: Managing Violent Covert Organizations*. Princeton: Princeton University Press.

Shapiro, Jacob, and Danielle Jung. 2014. "The Terrorist Bureaucracy: Inside the Files of the Islamic State in Iraq," *The Boston Globe*, December 14.

Sikkink, Kathryn. 2017. *Evidence for Hope: Making Human Rights Work in the 21st Century*. Princeton: Princeton University Press.

Smith, Nicholas Rush. 2017. "New Situations Demand Old Magic: Necklacing In South Africa, Past and Present," In Michael Pfeifer, ed., *Global Lynching and Collective Violence: Asia, Africa, and the Middle East*. Urbana: University of Illinois Press. Chapter 6, pp. 156–184.

Soifer, Hillel David. 2012. "Measuring State Capacity in Contemporary Latin America." *Revista de Ciencia Política* 32(3): 585–598.

Spruyt, Hendrik. 1994 *The Sovereign State and Its Competitors*. Princeton, NJ: Princeton University Press

Stewart, Meghan. 2018. "Civil War as State Building: Strategic Governance in Civil War." *International Organization* 72(1): 205–226.

Straus, Scott. 2007. "Second-generation Comparative Research on Genocide." *World Politics* 59(3): 476–501.

Steele, Abbey. 2011. "Electing Displacement: Political Cleansing in Apartadó, Colombia." *Journal of Conflict Resolution* 55(3): 423–445.

Thurston, Robert. 2011. "Lynching and Legitimacy: Toward a Global Description of Mob Murder." In *Globalizing Lynching History: Vigilantism and Extralegal Punishment from an International Perspective*, Manfred Berg and Simon Wendt, eds. New York: Palgrave Macmillan. Chapter 4, pp. 69–86.

Tolnay, Stewart Emory, and Elwood Beck. 1995. *A Festival of Violence: An Analysis of Southern Lynchings, 1882–1930*. University of Illinois Press.

US Army Field Manual 3–24: Counterinsurgency. 2006. FM 3–24/MCWP 3–33.5 www.hsdl.org/?abstract&did=468442

Valentino, Benjamin. 2005. *Final Solutions: Mass Killing and Genocide in the 20th century*. Ithaca: Cornell University Press.

Venkatesh, Sudhir. 1997. "The Social Organization of Street Gang Activity in an Urban Ghetto." *American Journal of Sociology* 29(4): 427–462.

Wagstaff, William, and Danielle Jung. 2018. "Competing for Constituents: Trends in Terrorist Service Provision" *Terrorism and Political Violence*. DOI:0.1080/09546553.2017.1368494.

Weber, Max. 1918. "Politics as a Vocation." In H. H. Gerth and C. Wright Mills (translated and edited), From Max Weber: Essays in Sociology. New York: Oxford University Press, 1946, pp. 77–128.

Weierstall, Roland, and Thomas Elbert. 2011. "The Appetitive Aggression Scale – Development of an Instrument for the Assessment of Human's Attraction to Violence." *European Journal of Psychotraumatology* 2(1): 8430.

Weintraub, Michael. 2016. "Legacies of Lynching: Racial Killings in the American South and Contemporary Homicides." Unpublished manuscript. Available by request from author.

Williams, Michael. 2006. "The Hobbesian Theory of International Relations: Three Traditions." In *Classical Theory in International Relations*, Beate Jahn, ed. New York: Cambridge University Press. Chapter 11, pp. 253–276.

Willman, Alys, and Louis Herns Marcelin. 2010. ""If They Could Make Us Disappear, They Would!" Youth and Violence in Cité Soleil, Haiti." *Journal of Community Psychology* 38(4): 515–531.

Yates, Donna. 2017. "Community Justice," Ancestral Rights, and Lynching in Rural Bolivia"; *Race and Justice*. https://doi.org/10.1177/2153368717713824.

Acknowledgements

The authors thank series editor David Stasavage for encouragement and feedback, and Michael Weintraub for detailed comments on the manuscript. We are grateful to Timothy Schwartz, Stephanie Pierre and the team at SocioDig, P. Anderson Soulouque, Almathe Jean, Garry Jerome, Richard Miguel and Jocelyne Colas Noël for sharing their guidance and expertise in Haiti, and to Pedro Braum, Jacqueline Charles, Arnaud Dandoy, Chris Fariss, Grant Gordon, Chelsey Kivland, Renard Sexton, Lynn Selby, Tara Slough, and Lauren Young for advice on research and practicalities in Haiti. We thank Ikapadata and Ikamva Youth for survey implementation in South Africa. Gray Barrett, Stefano Jud, and Kevin Sparrow provided terrific research assistance with the cross-national data collection and analysis. Danielle Villa was critical to assembling and translating the JILAP data on fatalities. Thanks also to Bridget Samburg for editing assistance, Tyler Simko for help with figures, and Mary Anne Baumgartner for superb support. We are grateful for critical comments from participants at the following workshops and seminars: the Ostrom Workshop at Indiana University, Columbia University International Politics Seminar, the Political Science seminar at NYU-Abu Dhabi and the Welfare Non-State Workshop at the University of California, San Diego. Jung is grateful for research support from Emory University. This research was made possible through generous support from the Folke Bernadotte Academy, and a number of research centers at Harvard University: the Belfer Center for Science and International Affairs, the Carr Center for Human Rights Policy, and the Women and Public Policy Program at the Harvard Kennedy School; and the Weatherhead Center for International Affairs, and the David Rockefeller Center for Latin American Studies. Finally, Cohen thanks Barry and Layla and Jung thanks her family and Leo for their many years of love and support.

Cambridge Elements ≡

Political Economy

David Stasavage

New York University

David Stasavage is Julius Silver Professor in the Wilf Family Department of Politics at New York University. He previously held positions at the London School of Economics and at Oxford University. His work has spanned a number of different fields and currently focuses on two areas: development of state institutions over the long run and the politics of inequality. He is a member of the American Academy of Arts and Sciences.

About the Series

The Element Series Political Economy provides authoritative contributions on important topics in the rapidly growing field of political economy.
Elements are designed so as to provide broad and in depth coverage combined with original insights from scholars in political science, economics, and economic history. Contributions are welcome on any topic within this field.

Cambridge Elements ☰

Political Economy

Elements in the Series

State Capacity and Economic Development: Present and Past
Mark Dincecco

Nativism and Economic Integration Across the Developing World: Collision and Accommodation
Rikhil R. Bhavnani and Bethany Lacina

Lynching and Local Justice: Legitimacy and Accountability in Weak States
Danielle F. Jung and Dara Kay Cohen

A full series listing is available at: www.cambridge.org/EPEC

Printed in the United States
By Bookmasters